Computing for Numerical Methods Using Visual C++ / Shahariddin Salleh,
Albert Y. Zomaya, and Sakhinah A. Bakar

Architecture-Independent Programming for Wireless Sensor Networks /
Amol B. Bakshi and Viktor K. Prasanna

ARCHITECTURE-INDEPENDENT PROGRAMMING FOR WIRELESS SENSOR NETWORKS

ARCHITECTURE-INDEPENDENT PROGRAMMING FOR WIRELESS SENSOR NETWORKS

Amol B. Bakshi
University of Southern California

Viktor K. Prasanna
University of Southern California

WILEY-INTERSCIENCE

A JOHN WILEY & SONS, INC., PUBLICATION

Published by John Wiley & Sons, Inc., Hoboken, New Jersey
Published simultaneously in Canada

For general information on our other products and services or for technical support, please contact
our Customer Care Department within the United States at (800) 762-2974, outside the United
States at (317) 572-3993 or fax (317) 572-4002.

Wiley also publishes its books in a variety of electronic formats. Some content that appears in print
may not be available in electronic formats. For more information about Wiley products, visit our
web site at www.wiley.com.

Library of Congress Cataloging-in-Publication Data:

Bakshi, Amol B., 1975-
  Architecture-independent programming for wireless sensor networks / Amol B. Bakshi, Viktor K. Prasanna.
    p. cm.
  Includes bibliographical references and index.
  ISBN 978-0-471-77889-9 (cloth)
  1. Sensor networks--Programming. 2. Wireless LANs--Programming. I. Prasanna Kumar, V. K. II. Title.
  TK7872.D48 B
  681'.2--dc22

                                                                              2007046862
Printed in the United States of America

10 9 8 7 6 5 4 3 2 1

CONTENTS

PREFACE

Networked sensing is an area of enormous research interest, as evidenced by the explosive growth of technical workshops, conferences, and journals related to topics in sensor networks as well as by the increasing number of related book publications. Research in sensor networks is influenced to varying degrees by ideas from traditional parallel and distributed computing, wireless ad hoc networking, signal processing, information theory, and so on. The semantics of spatial computing applications in sensor networks necessitate enhancements and extensions to traditional ideas in some cases and require the development of entirely new paradigms in others. The next generation of context-aware applications for these systems will require novel phenomenon-centric programming models, methodologies, and design tools to translate high-level intentions of the programmer into executable specifications for the underlying deployment. Indeed, such tools are critical for further development of the field; and once they become available, dramatic growth in this field can be expected.

This book deals with macroprogramming of networked sensor systems. A "macro"-programming language allows the application developer to express program behaviors at a high level of abstraction. The job of translating this high-level specification into node-level behaviors is delegated to a compilation and software synthesis system. Macroprogramming is interesting because it promises to facilitate rapid application development for large-scale, possibly heterogeneous sensor networks and also provides a framework for optimizing task placement and communication in such networks, without user involvement.

Objectives

We present a methodology and a programming language—called the Abstract Task Graph (ATaG)—for architecture-independent macroprogramming of networked sensor systems. Architecture-independence allows applications to be developed prior to decisions being made about the network deployment and also allows the same application to be compiled onto different target deployments.

ATaG is built upon two fundamental concepts: (1) the use of data-driven computing as the underlying control flow mechanism and (2) the adoption of mixed imperative-declarative notation for program specification. We argue that the former enables modular, composable programs for sensor networks and also provides an intuitive paradigm for specifying reactive behaviors in networked sensing. The latter separates concerns of task placement, firing, and in-network communication from the actual application functionality and is the key to architecture independence.

The objective of this book is to illustrate the feasibility and usefulness of architecture-independent programming for networked sensor systems. The discussion is centered around the ATaG model, which is discussed in detail. Ultimately, we want the reader to gain exposure to the high-level concepts that guided the design and implementation of the ATaG programming language and environment. We also discuss the implementation of the DART runtime system in great detail. This is because we want the reader to be familiar not just with the broad outline of DART but with its intimate details that will enable him/her to modify and/or extend the DART functionality as desired. Eventually, it is our hope that researchers can build upon ATaG and DART and design full-fledged compilation and code synthesis environments for a variety of networked sensor systems.

Book Organization

Chapter 1 provides a brief overview of sensor networks and the differences between sensor networks and traditional distributed systems. Various layers of programming abstraction for networked sensor systems are also reviewed, and the motivation for macroprogramming is discussed.

Chapter 2 presents the Abstract Task Graph (ATaG) model. A discussion of the ATaG syntax and semantics is followed by a section on programming idioms in ATaG. ATaG programs for oft-cited behaviors in networked sensing (hierarchical tree structures, object tracking, etc.) are presented.

Chapter 3 discusses the design of DART the Data-driven ATaG RunTime. An overview of the DART components is followed by an in-depth discussion of each component. Relevant code listings from the current implementation of DART accompany the discussion.

Chapter 4 outlines the overall process of application development with ATaG. This includes the graphical programming interface for ATaG, the automatic software synthesis mechanism, and the rudimentary compiler that translates ATaG programs into node-level behaviors. The simulation and visualization interface for ATaG is also discussed.

Chapter 5 presents an ATaG case study. In this chapter, we illustrate programming and synthesis of a composite application consisting of a gradient monitoring component and an object tracking component. We walk the reader through the steps involved in developing the declarative and imperative parts of the ATaG program and the software synthesis and rudimentary compilation support offered by the programming environment.

Chapter 6 concludes this book by discussing the broader context of the ATaG research. We argue that ATaG is not just a specific language for a class of sensor network applications but also a general framework that can be extended to a variety of behaviors in current and future sensor network applications. ATaG is also a framework for compilation in the sense that the syntax and semantics of ATaG and the design of the DART runtime system provide a well-defined framework for "intelligent compilation" of sensor network applications for a variety of target architectures.

Target Audience

This book is written for (i) researchers in networked embedded sensing and pervasive computing, (ii) researchers in parallel and distributed computing with applications to context-aware spatial computing, (iii) practitioners involved in implementing and deploying networked sensor systems, and (iv) application developers and software engineers for networked embedded systems for pervasive computing.

We particularly hope that the in-depth discussion of the design of the runtime system and of the simulation and visualization environment will enable interested researchers to download the software and use it to demonstrate extensions of the programming model or of the runtime system itself. To this end, we discuss specific extensions to ATaG and DART as future work in various clearly marked sections of this book.

AMOL B. BAKSHI
VIKTOR K. PRASANNA

Los Angeles, California
January, 2008

ACKNOWLEDGMENTS

The ATaG programming model and the associated programming environment was born in the summer of 2004 during the author Amol Bakshi's internship at the Palo Alto Research Center. Special thanks are due to Jim Reich and Dan Larner for co-inventing the programming model, as well as to Maurice Chu, Qingfeng Huang, Patrick Cheung, and Julia Liu for patient hearings and constructive feedback during the course of the summer work. We thank Prof. Ramesh Govindan and Prof. Bhaskar Krishnamachari (USC) for contributing broad perspectives on wireless networked sensing, specific inputs on the strengths and weaknesses of the ATaG model, and suggestions for future work.

We are grateful to Animesh Pathak and Qunzhi Zhou at the University of Southern California for their wholehearted adoption and ongoing furtherance of the ATaG research on macroprogramming for sensor networks. Finally, an enormous amount of gratitude is due to the wonderful—and wonderfully patient—people who encouraged this book project and drove it to completion: Prof. Albert Zomaya (Founding Editor-in-Chief of the Wiley Book Series on Parallel and Distributed Computing), Whitney Lesch, Val Moliere, Paul Petralia, Emily Simmons, Lisa Morano Van Horn, and Anastasia Wasko (Wiley); and Amy Hendrickson (TEXnology, Inc.).

A.B.B.
V.K.P.

CHAPTER 1

INTRODUCTION

Networked sensor systems

A networked sensor system (a "sensor network") is a distributed computing system where some or all nodes are capable of interacting with the physical environment. These nodes are termed as sensor nodes and the interaction with the environment is through sensing interfaces. Sensors typically measure properties such as temperature, pressure, humidity, flow, etc., when sampled. The sensed value can be one-dimensional or multi-dimensional. Sensor networks have a wide range of applications. Acoustic sensing can be used to detect and track targets in the area of deployment. Temperature, light, humidity, and motion sensors can be used for effective energy management through climate moderation in homes and commercial buildings.

Wireless sensor networks (WSNs) [44, 3, 17] are a new class of sensor networks, enabled by advances in VLSI technology and comprised of sensor nodes with small form factors, a portable and limited energy supply, on-board sensing, computing, and storage capability, and wireless connectivity through

Architecture-Independent Programming for Wireless Sensor Networks **1**
By Amol B. Bakshi, Viktor K. Prasanna
Copyright © 2008 John Wiley & Sons, Inc.

a bidirectional transceiver. WSNs promise to enable dense, long-lived embedded sensing of the environment. The unprecedented degree of information about the physical world provided by WSNs can be used for in situ sensing and actuation. WSNs can also provide a new level of context awareness to other back-end applications, making sensor networks an integral part of the vision of pervasive, ubiquitous computing—with the long-term objective of seamlessly integrating fine grained sensing infrastructure into larger, multi-tier systems.

There has been significant research activity over the last few years in the system-level aspects of wireless sensing. System level refers to the problems such as: (a) localization [41] and time synchronization [15, 16] to provide the basic "situatedness" for a sensor node node; (b) energy-efficient medium access protocols that aim to increase the system lifetime through means such as coordinated sleep–wake scheduling [60]; (c) novel routing paradigms such as geographic [33, 47], data-centric [22], and trajectory-based [40] that provide the basic communication infrastructure in a network where the assignment and use of globally unique identifiers (such as the IP addresses of the Internet) is infeasible or undesirable; (d) modular, component-based operating systems for extremely resource constrained nodes [27], etc. A variety of routing and data fusion protocols for generic patterns such as multiple-source single-sink data gathering trees are also being developed to optimize for a range of goodness metrics [30, 29, 61]. A comprehensive overview of state of the art in system level aspects of wireless embedded sensing can be found in [31, 18].

1.1 SENSOR NETWORKS AND TRADITIONAL DISTRIBUTED SYSTEMS

It is instructive to compare and contrast the fundamental nature of networked sensing with traditional parallel and distributed computing, with a view to identifying the degree to which the research in the latter field over the past few decades can be leveraged (with our without modification) to propose solutions for analogous problems in the former. Since the primary focus of this work is on models and methodologies for programming of large-scale networked sensor systems, the comparison will be biased towards aspects which influence application development and not so much on system level issues.

Sensor networks are essentially collections of autonomous computing elements (sensor nodes) that pass messages through a communication network and hence fit the definition of a distributed computing system proposed in [8]. However, some of the fundamental differences between networked sensor systems and traditional distributed computing systems are as follows:

Transformational versus reactive processing

The primary reasons for programming applications for a majority of traditional distributed computing systems were "high speed through parallelism, high reliability through replication of process and data, and functional specialization" [8]. Accordingly, the objective of most programming models and languages was to (i) allow the programmer to expose parallelism for the compiler and runtime system to exploit and (ii) provide support for abstractions such as shared memory that hide the distributed and concurrent nature of the underlying system from the application developer. In other words, the purpose of most abstractions was to allow the programmer to still visualize the target architecture as a von Neumann machine, which provided an intuitive and straightforward mental model of reasoning about sequential problem solving. Alternate approaches such as dataflow and functional programming were also proposed, motivated by a belief in the fundamental unsuitability of the von Neumann approach for parallel and distributed computing [5]. Regardless of the approach, most parallel and distributed applications were ultimately transformational systems that are characterized by a function that maps input data to output data. This function can be specified as a sequential, imperative program for a von Neumann architecture, and the purpose of parallelizing and distributing the execution over multiple nodes is mainly to reduce the total latency.

A networked sensor system is not a transformational system that maps a well-defined set of input data to an equally well-defined set of output data. Instead, like a majority of embedded software, it is a continuously executing and primarily reactive system that has to respond to external and internal stimuli [24]. An event of interest in the environment triggers computation and communication in the network. A quiescent environment ideally implies a quiescent network as far as application level processing is concerned.

Space awareness

An embedded sensor network can be considered to represent a discrete sampling of a continuous physical space. In fact, an abstract model of a distributed sensor network can be defined and analyzed purely in terms of measurements of the space being monitored [32], without any reference to the network architecture. In contrast to traditional distributed computing where all compute nodes were basically interchangeable and the physical location of a particular computing element is not directly relevant from a programming or optimization perspective, space awareness [63] is an integral part of embedded net-

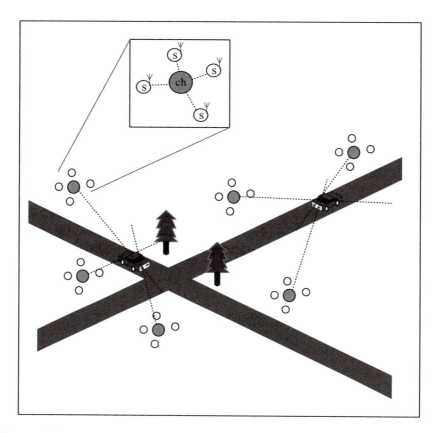

Figure 1.1   An example sensor network deployment for vehicle detection and tracking. Sensor nodes are deployed in clusters, with each cluster consisting of a relatively powerful clusterhead node and four resource-constrained sensor nodes. Each sensor could be equipped with acoustic and/or magnetic sensors. The individual sensor nodes in each cluster communicate their readings to the clusterhead which computes the line of bearing and possibly the type of vehicls. This information will be relayed to a supervisor station that can triangulate the object position by ending line of bearing estimates from multiple clusters. This particular scenario was one of the early use cases for wirelessly networked sensor systems.

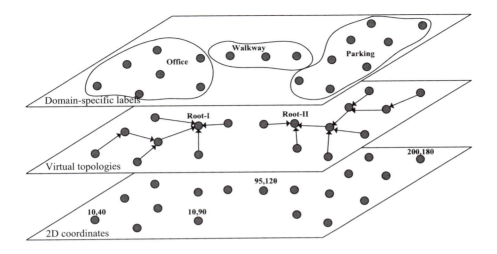

Figure 1.2   Multiple coordinate systems on the same deployment.

worked sensing. Most of the data in a sensor network deployment are created through the act of sampling the sensing interface(s), and the time and location of the sampling are in most cases a necessary part of the description of the sampled data. The spatio-temporal origin of a data item also affects the quality and quantity of processing performed on it.

Space awareness implies the existence of a coordinate system in which sensor nodes can be situated. In fact, a typical sensor network deployment is likely to have more than one coordinate system, each designed for a different purpose. For instance, the absolute or relative geographic coordinates might be required for tagging data samples at the node level, whereas the routing protocols could be using a different coordinate system that leads to reduced congestion and higher probability of timely data delivery in the network. Yet another coordinate system could be used for back-end processing which maps a particular (x, y) coordinate to, say, a building, a corridor, or a warehouse, depending on the application domain. Figure 1.2 depicts three coordinate systems overlaid on the same sensor network. From the perspective of application development for networked sensor systems, a real or virtual coordinate system can be deemed to be an essential service included in the system level infrastructure, the details of which need not concern the programmer.

Another aspect of space awareness is that the application behavior can be naturally specified in terms of spatial abstractions than in terms of nodes and edges of the network graph. For example, a temperature monitoring application can be specified as "if more than 70% of nodes within a 2-meter radius of any node report a temperature higher than 90 degrees, activate an alarm at that node location." The deployment of the network itself can be specified in terms of the desired degree of coverage. The exact placement of sensor nodes might not be of interest to the application developers as long as the set of sensing tasks mapped onto a subset of those nodes at any given time collaboratively ensures the desired coverage. Space-aware specification of the desired functionality is a unique aspect of networked sensor systems that has no analogous equivalent in traditional parallel and distributed computing.

Nature of input data

A majority of the data in a networked sensor system represents the occurrence of events in the physical environment and/or carries information about the events. Each data instance can be considered as a first-class entity with associated properties that could change with time and distance from its point of origin. For instance, in embedded sense-and-respond systems where sensing is coupled with local actuation and timely response to detected events is essential, the utility of the data that represent occurrence of the event reduces with time. If the data are not processed by the application within a certain duration from its time of origin, it is effectively useless. In-network processing that seeks to move the computation close to the source of the data is required in many sensor network applications to guarantee the desired end-to-end functionality. This is in contrast to traditional distributed computing, where the distribution of data and placement of tasks on compute nodes is primarily determined by performance and reliability considerations.

Also, different subsets of the total data in the network will be of interest to different applications at a given time, or to the same application at different times. In a sensor network deployed for climate moderation in a commercial building, an application component that periodically logs all temperature readings in a central database might not be interested in the semantics of that information, whereas another application component that is responsible for maintaining a uniform climate could be interested in temperature gradients that are above a certain threshold. From a programming perspective, it is important to give application developers the freedom to define what is relevant and what is irrelevant and to produce and consume data at the desired level of semantic abstraction.

The semantics of data could also influence the protocols and services used for transporting data through the network, and for prioritizing in-network activities that are triggered in response to certain events. A piece of data that represents a catastrophic event such as a forest fire is much more important than any other data in the network at that time and the computation and communication resources in the network can be expected to be devoted to expediting the transmission of the forest fire notification to its eventual destination. In a purely transformational system, however, it can be argued that the notion of importance of a particular piece of data does not really exist.

1.2 PROGRAMMING OF DISTRIBUTED SENSOR NETWORKS

1.2.1 Layers of programming abstraction

Figure 1.3 depicts our view of the emerging layers of programming abstraction for networked sensor systems. Many protocols have been implemented to provide the basic mechanisms for efficient infrastructure establishment and communication in ad hoc deployments. These include energy-efficient medium access, positioning, time synchronization, and a variety of routing protocols such as data-centric and geographic routing that are unique to spatial computing in embedded networked sensing. Ongoing research, such as MiLAN [26], is focusing on sensor data composition as part of the basic infrastructure. Sensor data composition essentially means that the responsibility of interfacing with physical sensors and aggregating the data into meaningful application-level variables is delegated to an underlying runtime instead of being incorporated as part of the application-level logic. We now discuss the layers of abstraction from the highest level of abstraction to the lowest.

1.2.1.1 Service-oriented specification   To handle the complexity of programming heterogeneous, large-scale, and possibly dynamic sensor network deployments and to make the computing substrate accessible to the non-expert, the highest level of programming abstraction for a sensor network is likely to be a purely declarative language. The Semantic Streams markup and query language [57] is an example of such a language that can be used by end users to query for semantic information without worrying about how the corresponding raw sensor data are gathered and aggregated. The basic idea is to abstract the collaborative computing applications in the network as a set of services and provide a query interpretation, planning, and resource management engine to translate the service requirements specified by the end

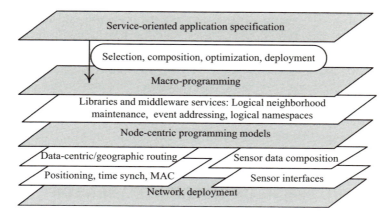

Figure 1.3 Layers of abstraction for application development on WSNs.

user into a customized distributed computing application that provides the result. A declarative, service-oriented specification allows dynamic tasking of the network by multiple users and is also easier to understand compared to low level distributed programming.

1.2.1.2 Macroprogramming The objective of macroprogramming is to allow the programmer to write a distributed sensing application without explicitly managing control, coordination, and state maintenance at the individual node level. Macroprogramming languages provide abstractions that can specify aggregate behaviors that are automatically synthesized into software for each node in the target deployment. The structure of the underlying runtime system will depend on the particular programming model. While service-oriented specification is likely to be invariably declarative, various program flow mechanisms—functional, dataflow, and imperative—are being explored as the basis for macroprogramming languages. Regiment [42] is a declarative functional language based on Haskell, with support for region-based aggregation, filtering, and function mapping. Kairos [23] is an imperative, control-driven macroprogramming language for sensor networks that allows the application developer to write a single centralized program that operates on a centralized memory model of the sensor network state. ATaG [6] (discussed in more detail in the remainder of this book) explores the dataflow paradigm as a basis for architecture-independent programming of sensor network applications.

```
1:  void buildtree(node root)
2:    node parent, self;
3:    unsigned short dist_from_root;
4:    node_list neighboring_nodes, full_node_set;
5:    unsigned int sleep_interval=1000;
    //Initialization
6:    full_node_set=get_available_nodes();
7:    for (node temp=get_first(full_node_set); temp!=NULL;
                        temp=get_next(full_node_set))
8:      self=get_local_node_id();
9:      if (temp==root)
10:       dist_from_root=0; parent=self;
11:     else dist_from_root=INF;
12:     neighboring_nodes=create_node_list(get_neighbors(temp));
13:   full_node_set=get_available_nodes();
14:   for (node iter1=get_first(full_node_set); iter1!=NULL;
                        iter1=get_next(full_node_set))
15:     for(;;) //Event Loop
16:       sleep(sleep_interval);
17:       for (node iter2=get_first(neighboring_nodes); iter2!=NULL;
                        iter2=get_next(neighboring_nodes))
18:         if (dist_from_root@iter2+1<dist_from_root)
19:           dist_from_root=dist_from_root@iter2+1;
20:           parent=iter2;
```

Figure 1.4   Kairos code example: Building a shortest path routing tree [23].

Figure 1.4 [23] is a complete, centralized Kairos program for building a shortest path routing tree from a root node that is an input parameter. The entire distributed algorithm for building such a tree is specified in this program. Note that this code is not directly executed on each node. Instead, it is parsed by a compiler that uses the program specification to (a) determine the actual code to generate for each of the nodes in the network and (b) manage the local and remote variables referred to in the code.

The initialization portion of the program gets all the nodes of the network, and for each node it sets the initial distance from root and the parent node pointer. The node that is to form the root of the routing tree sets its distance from root as zero and its parent pointer to itself, while all others set their distance to the root as infinity.

The event loop in lines 15 through 20 represents an iterative process where each node periodically contacts each of its one-hop neighboring nodes from the list of one-hop neighbors, determines if that node is closer to the root than itself, and conditionally sets its parent in the routing tree to the neighboring node that is nearest to the root.

```
let mesh = planarize world
    nodesAbove =
        afilter ((>= threshold) .
              (read_sensor SENSTYP))
              mesh
    midpoint nst1 nst2 =
        (read_nstate LOCATION nst1 +
         read_nstate LOCATION nst2) / 2
    contourpoints node =
        let neighborsBelow =
           filter ((< threshold) .
                   (read_nstate SENSTYP))
                   (get_neighbors node)
        in map (midpoint (get_nstate node))
               neighborsBelow
    all_contourpoints =
        amap contourpoints nodesAbove
 in
   afold append all contourpoints
```

Figure 1.5   Regiment code example: Determining the contour between adjacent areas of a sensor network [42].

Figure 1.5 [42] provides a glimpse into the Regiment programming style. The program shown in the figure determines the contour between adjacent areas of the network, where the nodes on one side of the contour have sensor readings above some threshold. The program, written as a functional language, first prunes the network graph into a planar form ("planarize world") and determines all the nodes whose sensor reading is above the threshold. The remainder of the code takes each node of the set of nodes above the threshold and forms a list of midpoints between the node and its neighboring nodes below the threshold. Finally, the list of midpoints generated at the contour nodes is aggregated to yield the contour line.

1.2.1.3 Node-centric programming   In node-centric programming, the programmer has to translate the global application behavior in terms of local actions on each node, as well as individually program the sensor nodes using languages such as nesC [19], galsC [13], C/C++, or Java. The program accesses local sensing interfaces, maintains application level state in the local memory, sends messages to other nodes addressed by node ID or location, and responds to incoming messages from other nodes. While node-centric programming allows manual cross-layer optimizations and thereby leads to

```
configuration Blink {
}
implementation {
  components Main, BlinkM, SingleTimer,
LedsC;

  Main.StdControl -> BlinkM.StdControl;
  Main.StdControl ->
SingleTimer.StdControl;
  BlinkM.Timer -> SingleTimer.Timer;
  BlinkM.Leds -> LedsC;
}
```

"configuration" file defines modules and wiring

```
interface StdControl {
  command result_t init();
  command result_t start();
  command result_t stop();
}
```

Interface definition file for StdControl

```
module BlinkM {
  provides {
    interface StdControl; }
  uses {
    interface Timer;
    interface Leds; }
}
implementation {
  command result_t StdControl.init() {
    call Leds.init();
    return SUCCESS; }
  command result_t StdControl.start() {
    return call Timer.start(TIMER_REPEAT, 1000) ; }
  command result_t StdControl.stop() {
    return call Timer.stop(); }
  event result_t Timer.fired() {
    call Leds.redToggle();
    return SUCCESS; }
}
```

Module definition implements interfaces and
uses interfaces from other modules included
in configuration file.

Figure 1.6   Programming in nesC.

efficient implementations, the required expertise and effort makes this approach insufficient for developing sophisticated application behaviors for large-scale sensor networks.

The concept of a logical neighborhood—defined in terms of distance, hops, or other attributes—is common in node-centric programming. Common operations upon the logical neighborhood include gathering data from all neighbors, disseminating data to all neighbors, applying a computational transform to specific values stored in the neighbors, etc. The usefulness and ubiquity of neighborhood creation and maintenance has motivated the design of node-level libraries [56, 55] that handle the low level details of control and coordination and provide a neighborhood API to the programmer.

Middleware services [26, 37, 62] also increase the level of programming abstraction by providing facilities such as phenomenon-centric abstractions. Middleware services could create virtual topologies such as meshes and trees in the network, allow the program to address other nodes in terms of logical, dynamic relationships such as leader–follower or parent–child, support state-centric programming models [35], etc. The middleware protocols themselves will typically be implemented using node-centric programming models and could possibly but not necessarily use communication libraries as part of their implementation.

1.2.2   Lessons from parallel and distributed computing

ATaG allows programmers to write architecture-independent networked sensing applications using a small set of application-neutral abstractions. Intuitive expression of reactive processing is accomplished in ATaG by using a data-driven paradigm, while architecture-independence is made possible through separation of functional concerns from the nonfunctional. These two core ideas have been explored in the distributed computing community. The data driven graph [52] extended the basic directed acyclic task graph model to support loop representation and dynamically created tasks in parallel programming. The use of data-driven semantics coupled with the task graph-like representation enabled clarity and simplicty of program design, and it also allowed for some optimizations relating to the data communication between tasks.

The benefits of separating the core application functionality from other concerns such as task placement and coordination motivated the FarGo [28] model that enabled dynamic layout of distributed applications in large-scale networks where capabilities of nodes and links could vary at runtime. By explicitly indicating co-location and re-location semantics of the tasks, FarGo elevated the performance and reliability of applications by allowing the deferment of layout decisions to runtime. Distributed Oz [25] is perhaps the closest to ATaG in terms of its objective of network transparency and network awareness. Distributed Oz cleanly separates the application functionality from aspects of distribution structure, fault tolerance, resource control and security, and openness. There are no explicit operations to transfer data across the network. All invocations of send() and receive() are done implicitly through language constructs of centralized programming. IBM's PIMA project [9] explored a "write once, run anywhere" model for application front-ends by specifying device-specific presentation hints separately from the tasks and their interactions – yet again highlighting separation of functional and nonfunctional concerns as the key enabler of architecture independence.

Tuple space is an abstract computation environment that represents a global communication buffer accessible to computational entities in the system. This was the basis for the generative communication model in the Linda coordination language [20] and is also being applied in networked sensing [14]. Communication orthogonality is a property of generative communication

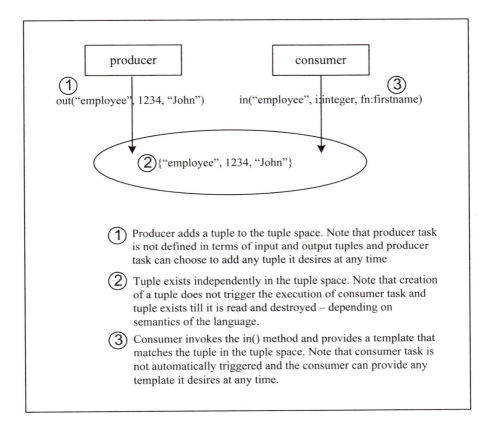

Figure 1.7   Programming with tuple spaces. The producer and consumer tasks communicate via "in" and "out" primitives. The tuple persists in the tuple spaces until it is actively retrieved by the consumer.

and means that both the sender and the receiver of a message are unaware of each other. ATaG also has this property because the tasks that produce and consume a particular data item in ATaG are not aware of each other. The data pool in ATaG is superficially similar to the notion of a tuple space. However, our active data pool moves the data items from producer to consumer(s) as soon as they are produced, and it schedules the consumer tasks based on their input interface and firing rules. This is different from the passive tuple space that merely buffers the produced data items and whose modifications are really a side effect of control-driven task execution.

In fact, the concept of tuple spaces has its roots in Blackboard architectures [43] of AI research. ATaG's active data pool is similar to the "demoned data servers" of DOSBART [34] that enabled distributed data-driven computation in a blackboard architecture. The notions of activity class and trigger activities of DOSBART are similar to the abstract tasks and their firing rules in the ATaG model, respectively.

1.3 MACROPROGRAMMING: WHAT AND WHY?

The primary focus of this dissertation is on the programming of large-scale networked sensor systems. The purpose of the typical sensor network deployment is to gather and process data from the environment for a single "end-to-end" objective. The program that executes on each node is part of a larger distributed application that delivers the results of an implicit or explicit domain specific query. Each node is required to be aware of its role in accomplishing the overall objective; that is, it is required to implement a predefined protocol for information exchange within the network. Consider a sensor network deployed for object tracking. The desired result of the implicit and perennial domain specific query in this case is the current location of target(s) (if any) in the network. A node-centric approach to programming the network requires each node to be programmed with the following behavior. The acoustic sensor is sampled periodically with a fixed or varying frequency, a Fourier transform is applied to the time-domain samples, and the result is compared with a set of acoustic patterns of interest to the end user. If a match is found, the time- and location-stamped result is communicated to a designated "clusterhead" node which performs further processing such as line of bearing estimation in an attempt to predict the location of the target.

This programming methodology where the desired global application behavior is manually decomposed by the programmer and subsequently coded into individual node-level programs is termed node-centric programming and is representative of state of the art. Node-centric programming has several limitations. Manual translation of global behavior into local actions is likely to be time-consuming and error prone for complex applications. If a new global behavior is to be added to an existing program, the modifications to the existing code are essentially ad hoc. The strong coupling of application-level logic and system-level services such as resource management, routing, localization, etc., also results in high coding complexity.

Macroprogramming broadly refers to programming methodologies for sensor networks that allow the direct specification of aggregate behaviors. The existence of a mechanism to translate the macroprogram into the "equivalent" set of node-level behaviors is implicit. The exact interpretation of macroprogramming varies. A Regiment program specifies operations (such as *fold* and *map*) over sensor data produced by nodes with certain geographic or topological relationships of interest. Since these subsets of the global network state can be manipulated as a single unit, Regiment is a macroprogramming language. Kairos is a macroprogramming language because the programmer writes a single, centralized program for the entire network, and the compiler and runtime system are responsible for the translation of this program into node-level behaviors, and implementing data coherence, respectively. TinyDB also enables macroprogramming because the programmer who formulates the SQL-like declarative aggregate query over sensor data is not responsible for (or even aware of) the details of in-network processing that are responsible for data collection and processing.

We define the following two types of macroprogramming that are supported by ATaG.

- *Application-level macroprogramming* means that the programming abstractions should allow the manipulation of information at the *desired* level of semantic abstraction. The information may indicate the occurrence of an event and/or also carry information about the occurrence. For instance, in an object tracking application, the program should be able to access information such as "number of targets currently tracked," "location of nearest target," etc., without worrying about how that information is obtained.

- *Architecture-level macroprogramming* means that the programming abstractions should allow concise specification of common patterns of distributed computing and communication in the network. Such patterns are represented as part of neighborhood libraries defined for node-centric programming methodologies [55]. These will typically have equivalent, concise abstractions in the macroprogramming language whose node-level implementation invokes the libraries.

A macroprogramming language can be application-neutral or application-specific. The *application-specific* approach entails customized language features to support a particular class of networked sensing applications. For example, a programming language explicitly designed for multi-target tracking might provide the current set of target locations or the handles to the current targets as a language feature whose implementation is hidden from the user. A language for temperature monitoring might provide a topographic map of the terrain as a built-in data structure that is created and maintained entirely by the runtime system. The advantage of this approach is that the implementation of domain-specific features can be optimized based on *a priori* knowledge of the pattern of information flow. If domain-specific features are integrated into the language, the resultant complexity of coding a behavior in that domain is also reduced. The drawback of this approach is that the portability and reusability of application-level code across network architectures, node architectures, and domains could be compromised. Also, adding new language features or modifying existing features might require a redesign of the runtime system and could be impossible or difficult for the application developer.

1.4 CONTRIBUTIONS AND OUTLINE

The two main contributions of this research are: (i) a **programming model** called the Abstract Task Graph (ATaG) for architecture-independent application development for a class of networked sensor systems and (ii) a component-based **software architecture for the runtime system**. A third contribution is a prototype environment for **visual programming** in ATaG and automatic **software synthesis** for the target network deployment. The prototype compiler integrated into this environment is designed to demonstrate functionally correct synthesis of a subset of the program features and does not optimize for any performance related metrics. Indeed, the definition of the compilation problem in the context of ATaG and the design and implementation of optimizing compilers for different scenarios is a significant research problem in its own right and one of the main areas of future work.

The Abstract Task Graph (ATaG)

ATaG is a macroprogramming model that builds upon the core concepts of data-driven computing and incorporates novel extensions for distributed sense-and-respond applications. In ATaG, the types of information processing functionalities in the system are modeled as a set of abstract tasks with well-defined input/output interfaces. User-provided code associated with each abstract task implements the actual processing in the system. An ATaG program is *abstract* because the exact number and placement of tasks and the control and coordination mechanisms are not defined in the program but are determined at compile-time and/or runtime, depending on the characteristics of the target deployment. Although ATaG is superficially based on the task graph representation, there are significant differences in the syntax and semantics, which arise from the requirements of distributed networked sensing. The differentiating factors include the notion of "abstract" tasks and data items, the use of data-driven program flow semantics of the graph, the elevation of data items as a first class entity in the graph representation along with the computational tasks, the concept of spatial scope of a directed edge, etc.

There is a growing interest in defining macroprogramming languages [23, 42] and application development environments [12, 53] for sensor networks. ATaG enables a methodology for architecture-independent development of networked sensing applications. The same ATaG program may be automatically synthesized for different network deployments, or adapted as nodes fail or are added to the system. Furthermore, it allows application development to proceed prior to decisions being made about the final configuration of the nodes and the network, and in future implementations it will permit dynamic reconfiguration of the application as the underlying network changes.

ATaG provides *application-neutral* support for macroprogramming. Using a small set of basic abstractions, ATaG allows programmers to define their own semantics for tasks and data items. The modularity and composability of ATaG programs means that a library of common behaviors in a particular domain can be defined by the programmer and can later be plugged into other applications that need not know the implementation details of the library component. This approach provides the benefits of using predefined domain-specific features while avoiding the restrictiveness of a domain-specific, custom built runtime system.

Data-Driven ATaG Runtime (DART)

ATaG is supported by a runtime system called DART whose structure and function is not visible to the programmer. DART has a component-based software architecture for modularity and flexibility. Each component of DART provides one or more well-defined services to other components. The implementation of a service is hidden from the users of the service. The current DART design can be easily implemented on operating systems that support preemptive priority-based scheduling, multi-threaded execution, mutual exclusion semaphores, message queues, and other mechanisms to handle concurrent access to critical sections and coordinate interactions between threads. Most traditional operating system kernels provide these facilities. A prototype version of DART has been implemented in Java, and is designed to run on relatively heavy duty sensor nodes, although Java Virtual Machines for resource-constrained architectures are also available [48]. DART is also being implemented on the μC/OS-II real-time OS kernel [39], which has been ported to a vast number of devices.

The performance of DART is unlikely to compare favorably with hand-optimized runtime systems where different functionalities are tightly integrated into an inflexible, monolithic structure, and many cross-layer optimizations are incorporated into the design. However, the tradeoff between usability and flexibility, on one hand, and hand-optimized performance, on the other, is common in all methodologies that seek to automate the design of complex systems. A greater level of experience with implementing different applications on a real DART-based system will guide future design choices for the ATaG runtime.

Software synthesis

In the context of the ATaG-based programming framework, software synthesis is the process of generating code for each node of the target sensor network deployment for the selected ATaG program. The code that is associated with each application-level functionality (abstract task) is to be provided by the programmer. The task of the software synthesis process is to generate the remainder of the software that is responsible for coordination and communication between the abstract tasks. To ease the task of software synthesis, we designed DART such that a majority of the code base either is agnostic to the application level functionality or can be customized by means of a configuration file that is generated by the software synthesizer. As an example, approximately 3000 lines of Java code runs on each sensor node in the ATaG program for object tracking (Section 2.5.1), of which only 100 lines are actually provided by the application developer and the rest is comprised of DART code that is used essentially unchanged and some glue code that is generated by the software synthesizer. The newly generated glue code is only 15 lines of Java that basically embeds the declarative part of the ATaG program into the runtime system, along with a one-line configuration file for each node in the target network that provides some state information to govern the node's behavior during the simulation.

Outline

The core ideas of ATaG have been individually explored in different contexts in the parallel and distributed computing community. There are also other approaches to the problem of macroprogramming of sensor networks being explored in the sensor networking community. Some of these were discussed previously in this chapter. Chapter 2 presents the ATaG programming model in detail with a description of a syntax and semantics of ATaG program. A set of programming idioms are also provided to illustrate the formulation of oft-cited behaviors in sensor networking as ATaG programs. The design of the DART runtime system is the subject of Chapter 3, which describes the service provided by each of the DART components, the interactions between the various components, and implementation notes. Chapters 2 and 3 also include a discussion of future research directions in the context of the programming model and the design of the runtime system, respectively. Chapter 4 presents the visual programming and software synthesis environment for ATaG. A brief primer on the Generic Modeling Environment [21] precedes the discussion of the various modeling paradigms that are provided to the application developer. A case study is included in Chapter 5 to illustrate the development of an application consisting of two behaviors—object tracking and environment monitoring—using this programming environment. We conclude in Chapter 6.

CHAPTER 2

THE ABSTRACT TASK GRAPH

2.1 TARGET APPLICATIONS AND ARCHITECTURES

ATaG is not designed for a particular sensor node platform, network architecture, or application domain. We model the deployment as a distributed
system consisting of a set of autonomous elements (sensor nodes). Each element of the system has on-board computation and storage capability and can
communicate with the rest of the elements through one or more neighbors. In
addition, each element may be equipped with one or more types of sensing
or actuation mechanisms that can be controlled through software. Since situatedness (localization) is fundamental to embedded networked sensing, we
assume that each element is capable of determining its own location in some
shared coordinate system and/or namespace.

The programming model makes no assumptions about the communication
interface (wired or wireless) or about the computation, storage, and energy
resources available to a node. Of course, the resources at a node will constrain

By Amol B. Bakshi, Viktor K. Prasanna

the number of tasks that can be mapped onto it, the latency of communication could be affected by the available bandwidth between the node and its neighbors, and the type of energy resources available could also affect the system-wide performance. This analysis is expected to be performed at compile time in the context of a specific network architecture, and the suitability of an ATaG program for a particular architecture is not meant to be inherent in the program itself. Thus, the target system can encompass a heterogeneous collection of micro-sensor nodes such as the Motes, more capable nodes such as the Stargate, and even desktop PCs or servers connected to the internet. ATaG also makes no assumptions about the mobility of nodes or other factors that could lead to changes in network topology at run time. The interpretation of program elements will depend on the nature of the target deployment, but the definition of the features of the programming model is independent of such assumptions.

For example, an ATaG programmer can specify the instantiation density of an application level task and can state, say, that one instance of task A should be instantiated per square meter of the deployment. In this case, if the nodes are mobile, the runtime system is expected to be capable enough to detect situations when this requirement is no longer satisfied and take corrective measures such as reassigning tasks to nodes in a way that expected density is once again achieved. If the nodes are immobile, the initial task assignment at compile time can be expected to be valid until other factors such as energy depletion necessitate reassignment. In this example, the application developer does not care about the static or dynamic nature of the deployment as long as the high-level application requirements as expressed through an ATaG program are met. More important, keeping the programming model free of such assumptions also adds to the architecture independence of the application. Of course, this does not preclude ATaG programs from being designed for specific types of deployments, but the programming model itself is designed for a range of network architectures, with the job of deployment-specific customization largely delegated to the compilation process and the protocols and services incorporated into the underlying runtime system.

ATaG programs are data-driven, which means that tasks are scheduled when their data are available (possibly also subject to other firing rules). Tasks interact only with the data pool, and one task cannot directly control other tasks. This lack of application-level control over task scheduling and execution (that is entirely managed by the underlying runtime system) limits the applicability of ATaG to scenarios where such fine-grained control over node-level execution is not required. Low-duty cycle environment monitoring that require periodic network-wide data collection with or without in-network aggregation is an example of an application that can be programmed in ATaG. On the other hand, if an application requires strict latency guarantees on critical paths from sensing to actuation, a control-driven programming language such as Kairos [23] may be better suited than the data-driven semantics of ATaG.

2.2   KEY CONCEPTS

ATaG is based on two key concepts: (i) data-driven program flow that enables intuitive expression of reactive processing in the network and leads to modular, composable, and reusable programs and (ii) mixed imperative-declarative program specification that separates the functional and non-functional aspects of the application and provides architecture independence, spatial awareness, and network awareness. We discuss these concepts in more detail in the following subsections.

2.2.1   Data-Driven Computing

2.2.1.1   Program flow mechanisms   Three basic program flow mechanisms being explored in the context of programming of networked sensor systems are: control-driven, data-driven, and demand-driven. In **control-driven** program flow, instructions are executed in an explicitly specified order. An example of this is the well-known von Neumann architecture where the program counter is incremented (or otherwise modified) after every execution and the next instruction in the sequence is decoded and executed. The single thread of control passes from instruction to instruction, and the modifications to the data store are a side effect of instruction execution. Data are passed indirectly between instructions by means of referencing common memory locations. In parallel forms of control flow, there are multiple threads and mechanisms such as fork and join for coordination between the threads. Imperative languages such as C are representative of control-driven programming. Paradigms such as object-oriented programming, distributed programming through message passing, etc., provide ways to structure complex control-driven programs to make them easier to design, maintain, and/or deploy, but the basic model of a set of "active" instructions manipulating a (conceptually) shared "passive" data store remains unchanged.

Data-driven program flow is fundamentally different from control-driven flow in the following aspects. First, the flow of control is governed by data dependencies and not determined by an explicitly specified sequence of tasks/in-

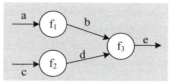

The computation:
$b = f_1(a); d = f_2(c); e = f_3(b,d)$

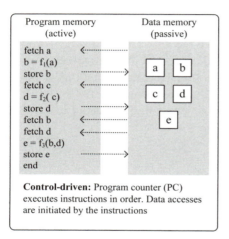

Control-driven: Program counter (PC)
executes instructions in order. Data accesses
are initiated by the instructions

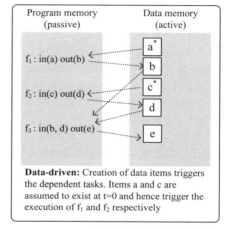

Data-driven: Creation of data items triggers
the dependent tasks. Items a and c are
assumed to exist at t=0 and hence trigger the
execution of f_1 and f_2 respectively

Figure 2.1   Data-driven vs. Control-driven.

structions to be executed. Tasks are defined in terms of their input and output
data items. In the basic dataflow model, an instruction is considered to be
enabled when its operands are ready, and the program terminates when no
instructions are enabled. Data dependence is the sole means of task scheduling and also the synchronization. Second, data are explicitly passed between
tasks. There is a data pool abstraction that tasks write to and read from, but
the concept of indirect sharing of data through referencing common locations
(shared variables) in the data pool does not exist. Dataflow programs are
commonly expressed as directed graphs where the nodes of the graph correspond to tasks (instructions) and the directed arrows denote data dependencies
between tasks.

The term "event-driven processing" is used in the sensor network community, specifically in the context of the TinyOS operating system for the
Berkeley Motes. Event-driven means that processes need not poll or block

for input, consuming valuable system resources while doing so. In networked sensor systems where certain kinds of events might be very rare compared to the frequency of polling, such behavior is wasteful. Instead, the event-driven philosophy allows the process to sleep until its required trigger input is available and be woken up (activated) at the suitable time. Programming with the nesC language qualifies as event-driven programming because the program is basically structured as a set of modules with well-defined interfaces that can be invoked by other modules to request a service ("commands") or act as a callback to the caller module to indicate completion of the service ("events"). The event-driven execution in this context is essentially control-driven program flow where the events correspond not to the availability of input data for a particular module, but to the invocation of an asynchronous function call by another module. The transfer of data between modules (if any) is hidden in the arguments to the function being invoked. The core of the operating system is just a scheduler, and there is no active data store that spawns tasks based on their firing conditions.

Tuple spaces is another abstraction that is superficially similar to data-driven program flow but, at least as used in the Linda coordination language, is basically a mechanism for spatially and temporally decoupled sharing of data among multiple processes in a control-driven distributed program. A tuple space is a shared, associative memory maintained by an underlying run-time system. Although the shared memory abstraction reduces the complexity of distributed programming compared to message passing, location-based addressing of the shared memory is cumbersome for a variety of reasons. Instead, processes add "tuples" to the shared memory by means of an in() primitive, and they read tuples by means of the out() primitive. Tuples are typed groupings of relevant fields that are addressed not by their location in the logically shared memory but by their content and type. Since the reads and writes are directed at the tuple space and not at other processes, programs gain modularity and extensibility. The tuple space can be considered as just another form of shared memory in a control-driven program flow because the thread of control is very much in the processes themselves and not determined by the contents of the tuple space. Like the event-driven programming of nesC/TinyOS which eliminates the need for polling or blocking and thereby makes control-driven programming more efficient, mechanisms such as the notify() primitive of JavaSpaces have been defined for the tuple space abstractions. However, just as event-driven execution does not make nesC a data-driven language, the addition of notify() to tuple spaces does not make it a data-driven paradigm, although the other benefits of the tuple spaces make it a promising approach for sharing information in highly distributed and dynamic systems such as sensor networks. One of the many extensions to the basic Linda model that have been proposed over the past couple of decades is Lime, which, among other extensions, adds the concept of a reaction, which is a method to be executed when a tuple matching a particular pattern is found among the contents of the tuple space. An overview, classification, and analysis of approaches to embed reactive processing in shared dataspaces can be found in [11].

Finally, demand-driven programming—also known as reduction programming—is a third paradigm where the demand for a value triggers the computation that is responsible for producing the value. That computation may in turn require values that lead to more computations and so on. Functional programming with lazy evaluation is an example of the demand-driven program flow mechanism. In reduction programs, there is typically no concept of a storage location that can be read and written. All program structures are expressions. When a program is expressed as a function whose arguments in turn can be functions themselves, the programmer is describing the solution space without specifying the exact sequence of instruction execution required to arrive at a solution. Regiment [42] is a functional language based on Haskell that exploits the declarative nature of functional programming to simplify the task of collaborative computing in networked sensor systems.

2.2.1.2 Why data-driven?

The individual sensor node will typically have a traditional, sequentially programmable von Neumann or Harvard architecture, along with support for one or more control-driven, imperative languages such as C. At the system level, which is the domain of macroprogramming, there are different ways of modeling the collection of von Neumann architectures that forms the overall computing substrate. One approach is to (a) extend the node-level programming paradigm to encompass the entire system and (b) model the sensor network as a single processing element and a single centralized memory [23]. The von Neumann model can also be abandoned at the system level altogether, and the macroprogramming language can be based upon an alternate paradigm such as functional programming [42]. ATaG explores the dataflow paradigm for the following reasons.

Reactive processing. A sensor network application can be intuitively modeled as a set of node-level or system-level responses to node-level or system-level events. Events will be defined by the application developer at desired levels of semantic abstraction, based on the application domain. An event could indicate the occurrence of phenomena in the physical environment (physical event) or the execution of a particular phase of processing in the network (computational event). In addition to denoting occurrence, the event could also carry information about (a) the phenomena in the former case and (b) the results of intermediate computation in the latter. Similarly, a reaction to an event could involve a sequence of computation and communication involving one or more nodes of the network.

Data-driven programming is especially suited for expressing reactive applications. A data-driven program consists of a set of tasks with well-defined input and output interfaces. In the pure data-driven model, a task is executed only when all of its inputs are available. However variants of the basic model (including our variant in ATaG) allow the definition of firing rules that can be used to define triggering condition of a task. For instance, a task could be triggered when a specific input is available, or when any one of its inputs is available, or when a certain fraction of its inputs are available. These basic rules can be used to define complex behaviors, as will be illustrated in Section 2.5. Also, tasks are disjoint from each other in the sense that all interaction between tasks is indirect—through the production and consumption of data items. Since tasks are decoupled, a given task can defined to use data items at the desired level of semantic abstraction without having to worrying about how they are produced. This supports application-level macroprogramming.

Reusability and composability. Modularity, reusability, and composability are important nonfunctional requirements for sensor network applications. Ultimately, we envision our programming model to be integrated into an application synthesis framework similar to the vision of service-oriented program composition [36]. Macroprograms will be generated automatically from a high-level declarative specification and in turn compiled into node-level specifications. Modularity and composability enables the creation of libraries of commonly encountered behaviors and allows existing applications to be suitably reused as subsets of larger functionalities.

In control-driven distributed programming using message passing or other communication libraries, tasks explicitly invoke each other's services. Since this requires a task to have information about other task it communicates with, any modification to a task is likely to affect other tasks in the program. Also, if a new task (functionality) is added to the program, all tasks that are to take advantage of that functionality must be modified to incorporate the suitable calls to the newly added task. This tight coupling of task interfaces restricts the reusability of code and composability of programs.

In data-driven programming however, task interfaces are specified as "Task A reads data item Temperature and produces data item Alarm" or "Task B reads data item Temperature and produces data item Maximum." Suppose a new functionality is to be added to this temperature monitoring program. The purpose of this new task is to corroborate the readings from a wider area around the node that produced the alarm and produce another "verified alarm" based on the results. In data-driven programming, all that is required is to simply define a new task as "Task C reads data items Alarm and Temperature and produces data item VerifiedAlarm." The representation of the spatial aspect of this processing will be discussed in the next section, specifically the collection of data from the neighborhood. The emphasis here is on the fact that the addition of Task C does not change the existing tasks in any way. Also, Task C does not care about how the Alarm is produced by Task B. The new program is simply a concatenation of the three tasks, and their mutual dependency is implicit in their input and output interfaces defined in terms of data items.

2.2.2 Mixed Imperative–Declarative Specification

Imperative programming is a programming paradigm where computation is specified in terms of statements (commands) that are to be executed in sequence and that change the program state. Almost all processors are designed to execute imperative programs, and the program state at any given time is represented by the contents of the processor memory at that time. Since imperative programming requires the programmer to specify the 'how' of computation in detail, the advantage of intimate control over program execution is offset by the programming complexity, especially for large-scale and/or distributed systems. High-level procedural languages and object-oriented languages provide constructs such as objects that ease the task of writing complex imperative programs, but the basic paradigm remains unchanged. nesC [19] and Kairos [23] are examples of imperative programming languages for sensor network applications.

Declarative programming, in contrast, focuses on the "what" of computation, leaving the "how" unspecified. A declarative program can be viewed as the description of a solution space where the sequence of steps to arrive at the solution is left to some underlying interpreter. Functional programming and logic programming are examples of declarative programming. The major advantage of declarative programming from an application development perspective is the reduced complexity of programming that is a result of delegating most of the selection and synthesis of underlying mechanisms to an unspecified interpreter, while the application developer focuses primarily on formulating the solution space. Regiment [42], TinyDB [38], and Semantic Streams [57] are examples of the declarative programming paradigm for sensor network applications.

Now, the functional aspect of a sensor network application refers to the code (tasks) that runs on the individual sensor nodes and performs data processing. Examples of nonfunctional aspects are task placement and mechanisms for communication and coordination. Consider a simple application where a collector task running on a designated root node periodically receives and logs temperature readings from every node in the network. The functional aspects of this application are completely defined by the code that performs the sampling and the code that performs the logging. As long as there is a mechanism to (i) ensure the placement of one sampling task on each node of the network and one logging task on the root node, (ii) periodically execute the sampling task, and (iii) route the sampled data from its point of origin to the root node, the details of its implementation should not be the application developers' concern.

The ATaG programming paradigm is based on the observation that specification of functional aspects of the networked sensing application in an imperative style and the nonfunctional aspects in a declarative style affords a tradeoff between the need for control over application execution and the need to reduce the complexity of communication and coordination. The latter is a substantial fraction of a networked sensing application and can really be considered as a service offered by the system instead of an integral and integrated part of the application code.

More importantly, ATaG enables architecture independence by clearly separating the "when and where" of processing from the "what." The former constitutes the *declarative* part and is specified through parameterized spatial and temporal attributes for a generic network architecture. The latter constitutes the *imperative* part and is the actual task code supplied by the user. The same program can be compiled for a different network size and topology by interpreting the declarative part in the context of that network architecture while the imperative part remains unchanged.

2.3 SYNTAX

2.3.1 The Structure of an ATaG program

The *task graph* is a widely used application model. In the task graph notation, the overall computation is represented as an acyclic directed graph. The nodes of the graph correspond to processes (tasks), and a pair of distinct tasks are connected by a directed edge iff the task at the tail of the directed edge requires as input the results of execution of the task at its head. In the simplest model, a task cannot start executing until all its predecessors have finished execution. For transformational applications, the task graph exposes the potential for concurrent execution of tasks and is widely used in task scheduling and allocation [2, 45]. The task graph is also commonly annotated/extended with other information relevant to the problem domain—for example, the conditional task graph for low-power embedded system synthesis [58], the augmented task dependency graph [46] for automated software partitioning and mapping for distributed multiprocessors, the iterative task graph for representing loops [59], etc. Annotation of paths in the task graph with throughput and latency constraints has been employed for resource allocation in distributed sensor–actuator systems [4].

The ATaG model of a program is similar to the task graph model in that the application is represented as a set of tasks and a set of data items connected via directed arrows denoting the input or output relationship between a task and a data item. Tasks and arrows (called "channels" in ATaG) also have associated annotations that determine the translation of the architecture-independent ATaG program in the context of a particular network deployment.

An ATaG program is a set of *abstract declarations*.   An abstract declaration can be one of three types: *abstract task*, *abstract data*, or *abstract channel*. Each abstract declaration consists of a set of *annotations*. Each annotation is a 2-tuple where the first element is the *type* of annotation, and the second element is the *value*. Hereafter, we occasionally omit the word "abstract" for sake of brevity. Figure 2.2 provides a general overview of the

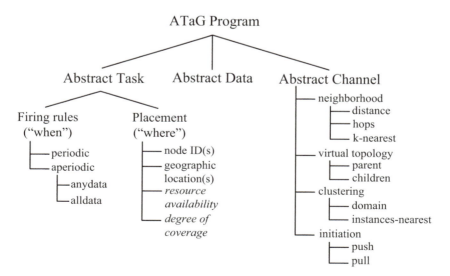

Figure 2.2   An overview of the ATaG syntax.

ATaG syntax and the broad classification of the annotation types currently supported. The task annotations relate to the placement and firing rules of tasks, while the channel annotations are used to specify different types of "interests" in instances of the associated abstract data item. Support for task placement based on compile-time or runtime availability of resources or on the desired degree of coverage (for sensing tasks) is not yet implemented in the prototype ATaG programming environment, and is hence italicized in the figure. The set of annotations is open-ended: More types can be defined based on the target class of applications, the hardware architecture of the sensor node, and the capabilities of the runtime system.

Abstract task: Each abstract task declaration represents a type of processing that could occur in the application. The number of instances of the abstract task existing in the system at a given time is determined in the context of a specific network description by the annotations associated with that declaration. Each task is labeled with a unique name by the programmer. Associated with each task declaration is an executable specification in a traditional programming language that is supported by the target platform. Table 2.1 describes the annotations that can be associated with a task declaration in the current version of ATaG.

Abstract data: Each abstract data declaration represents a *type* of application-specific data object that could be exchanged between abstract tasks. ATaG does not associate any semantics with the data declaration. The number of instances of a particular type of data object in the system at a given time is determined by the associated annotations in the context of a specific deployment and depends on the instantiation and firing rules of tasks producing or consuming the data objects. Each data declaration is labeled with a unique *name*. Similar to the executable code associated with the task declaration, an application-specific *payload* is associated with the data declaration. This payload typically consists of a set of variables in the programming language supported by the target platform. No other annotations are currently associated with abstract data items.

Abstract channel: The abstract channel associates a task declaration with a data declaration and represents not just which data objects are produced and/or consumed by a given task, but which instances of those types of data items are of interest to a particular instance of the task. An abstract channel is called an input (output) channel if the data item is to be consumed (produced) by the task. In an ATaG program, more than one input channels may be defined for a given abstract data item—denoting the fact that more than one consumer exists

Table 2.1 Abstract Task: Annotations.

Type: Instantiation

Value[:Parameter]	Description
one-anywhere	Create one instance of the task on any node in the network
one-on-node-label:*l*	Create one instance of the task on each node labeled *l* (dynamic)
one-on-node-ID:*id*	Create one instance of the task on node *id*
nodes-per-instance:[/]*n*	Create one instance of the task for each *n* nodes of the network. When *n* is preceded by a "/", create exactly *n* instances of the task and divide the total number of nodes into *n* non-overlapping domains, each owned by one instance.
area-per-instance:[/]*area*	Same as for nodes-per-instance. Parameter denotes area of deployment instead of number of nodes. The non-overlapping domains are in terms of area of deployment, not number of nodes.
spatial-extent:$x_1, y_1, x_2, y_2, \ldots$	Create one instance of the task on every node that is deployed in the polygon defined by the coordinates $(x_1, y_1), (x_2, y_2), \ldots, (x_1, y_1)$.

Type: Firing rule

Value[:Parameter]	Description
periodic:*p*	Schedule task for periodic execution with period of *p* seconds.
any-data	Schedule task for execution when at least one of the input data items are available.
all-data	Schedule task for execution only when all the input data items are available.

for that type of data. The current design of the ATaG runtime allows only one output channel to be associated with a particular abstract data item; that is, there can be at most one producer task. This restriction may be eliminated in the future.

Table 2.2 describes the annotations that can be associated with an abstract channel in the current version of ATaG. The abstract channel is the key to concise, flexible, and architecture-independent specification of common patterns of information flow in the network. For instance, spatial dissemination and collection patterns may be expressed using simple annotations such as "1-hop," "local," or "all nodes," on output and input channels. More sophisticated annotations may be defined as needed or desired for a particular application

Table 2.2   Abstract Channel: Annotations.

Type: Initiation

Value	Description
push	The runtime system at the site of production of each instance of the associated abstract data item is responsible for sending the instance to nodes hosting suitable instances of the consumer task(s).
pull	The runtime system at the node hosting an instance of the consumer task is responsible for requesting the required instance(s) of the associated abstract data item from the site(s) of production.

Type: Interest

Value[:Parameter]	Description
[¬]local	Channel applies to the local data pool of the task instance. The negation qualifier excludes the local data pool, and can be used in conjunction with other qualifiers (see Section 2.3.3 for an example).
neighborhood-hops:n	Channel includes all nodes within the n-hop neighborhood of the node hosting the task instance
neighborhood-distance:d	Channel includes all nodes within a distance d of the node hosting the task instance
k-nearest-nodes:k	Channel includes the k nearest nodes of the node hosting the task instance
k-nearest-pc:k	The input (output) channel includes the the set of nodes that host the k nearest producers (consumers) of the data item associated with this channel
all	Channel includes all nodes in the system
domain	Channel includes all nodes that are owned by the task instance. This value is used in conjunction with the nodes-per-instance or area-per-instance values of the Instantiation annotation of the abstract task (see Fig. 2.10 for an example)
parent	Channel applies to the parent of the node hosting the task instance; in the virtual tree topology imposed on the network by the runtime system.
children	Channel applies to all children of the node hosting the task instance; in the virtual tree topology imposed on the network by the runtime system.

domain. Section 2.5 illustrates the application of these annotations through a set of ATaG programming examples.

In the following sections, we discuss in more detail the task and channel annotations listed in Tables 2.1 and 2.2, respectively. The annotations in the tables are a representative subset defined to illustrate the specification of oft cited programming idioms in current sensor networking literature using the ATaG model. There is no fixed (standard) set of annotations for ATaG. In fact, the annotations that form the declarative part of ATaG programming can and should be customized to different application domains and system architectures.

2.3.2 More on task annotations

The essence of mixed imperative–declarative specification is the separation of task functionality from the conditions that govern the instantiation of that functionality on one or more nodes of the network at a given time. The need to specify where (spatial) and when (temporal) such instantiation should occur leads to two classes of task annotations: The first is related to placement (spatial) and the second specifies the firing rules (temporal). Annotations in these two classes govern spatial and temporal task instantiation, respectively.

Task placement versus task invocation. The placement of a task on a particular node does not necessarily mean that it will be invoked. The invocation depends on the satisfaction of firing rules on that node. For instance, in a fire monitoring application, each node could host a task that is responsible for sending an alarm message containing the location of a fire detected in the node's neighborhood. The placement annotation for this task will specify that it should be instantiated on all nodes. The firing rule for this task will indicate that it should be invoked only when certain conditions are satisfied. In a data-driven programming model like ATaG, this condition will typically be the presence of a data object that is produced by one or more other tasks on the node or on the neighboring nodes only when the result of the collaborative computation on temperature reading indicates the likelihood of a fire.

Although the alarm notification task is placed on each node of the network, only a small fraction of the tasks may actually be executed in the lifetime of the sensor network. This distinction between placement and invocation, along with the fact that the former does not necessarily imply the latter, is therefore important.

Task placement versus code placement. Another related issue is that of task placement versus code placement. The abstract task of an ATaG application is a unit of functionality that is flexibly instantiated in the network. When an ATaG application is compiled onto a target deployment, the placement annotations for the abstract tasks are interpreted in the context of the target network and the tasks are "assigned to" or "placed onto" a subset of the nodes. Code placement, on the other hand, refers to the presence of the code corresponding to that task in the program memory of that node. This distinction becomes important for sensor networks where the program memory is relatively large and every sensor node has enough storage to host the code associated with every abstract task in the ATaG application, regardless of whether that task is assigned to (or placed on) that node. Just as task placement does not necessarily imply task invocation, code placement does not necessarily imply task placement in this resource-rich sensor network scenario.

In resource-constrained environment, code placement could correspond to task placement and the application-level code provided to a node will be only for the tasks that are placed onto that node. If one or more tasks have to be re-assigned to adapt to a changing network or changing application requirements, the necessary code will also have to be provided to nodes that previously did not host the task. In resource-rich environments where the node already has the code for all tasks in the applications, reassignment can be performed much more simply by setting a flag in the runtime system to record the assignment of the task to the node. The ATaG programming model is independent of the architecture of the target network or sensor node. The application development methodology with ATaG allows for the same ATaG program to be compiled into widely varying architectures by encapsulating the architecture-specific translations within a compiler. Multiple compilers can be plugged into the ATaG application development environment and can conceptually allow the same program to be compiled for different architectures from a single programming and software synthesis environment.

We now discuss the placement annotations in more detail. The annotations listed in Table 2.1 can be broadly divided into three subclasses: (i) fine-grained control over task placement, (ii) density-based instantiation, and (iii) geographic instantiation. These subclasses are not exclusive and a given annotation could belong to more than one of these classes.

Fine-grained control over task placement. In some applications, the location of certain types of functionality is predetermined. For instance, consider an in-building climate control system that is monitored from some central station. Besides the in-network sense-and-response functionality, periodic status reports could be forwarded to the central station that is also abstracted as a sensor node. Now, the location and/or identifier of this supervisor node are determined at design time, and the supervisor task in the application must be assigned to this node. In scenarios such as these, there needs to be a way for the programmer to indicate the exact placement of one or more tasks based on *a priori* knowledge of the sensor network deployment. The one-on-node-ID:n is an example of an annotation that provides such fine grained control over task placement. Currently, the parameter for this annotation is the node ID, with the assumption that each node in the network has a unique identifier that is known at compile time. This annotation can be trivially generalized to allow the specification of a list of node IDs instead of a single ID, thereby allowing the programmer to specify a list of nodes that should host the task in question.

The spatial extent:x1,y1,x2,y2,... annotation has a similar motivation and capability as the one-on-node-ID:n annotation, except that the former allows fine-grained placement control in terms of geographic area. For deployment scenarios where the (real or virtual) coordinate system is known *a priori*, this annotation can be used to localize certain applications to a specific area of deployment, thereby enabling a virtual partitioning of the deployment into different zones. For instance, a particular spatial extent might correspond to a parking garage, whereas another extent could map onto an adjacent office building. Although a single, connected sensor network could encompass both the office building and the parking garage, the programmer might be interested in deploying, say, a vehicle speed monitoring application only in the parking garage and not in the office building.

Density-based instantiation. Density-based instantiation is based on the observation that a sensor network can be modeled as a discrete sampling of a continuous physical space. The "end user" who is interested in obtaining information about properties or events of interest in the physical environment will not be overly concerned with the number of nodes in the network, their connectivity, placement, etc. The types of sensing interfaces and the range of the sensors are likely to be of greater interest than the radio range and the network connectivity. In other words, if the range of a particular sensing interface is, say, one square meter, instantiating the corresponding task with an approximate density of one square meter should be sufficient to guarantee a high degree of coverage. Depending on the density of the node deployment, this specification could translate into an instantiation density in terms of nodes. From the programmers' perspective, however, the former specification captures the high-level intent independent of a particular network architecture. Hence, annotations such as "area-per-instance:area" have been defined. The "nodes-per-instance:n" annotation provides a similar control over instantiation density but in terms of sensor nodes instead of area.

Task assignment to logical partitions. Variants of the density-based instantiation annotations are created by inserting a "/" before the parameter value. The area-per-instance:/n annotation instructs the compiler to divide the total area of deployment into exactly n domains and to place one instance of the task in each domain. Similarly, the nodes-per-instance:/n annotation implies a partitioning of the number of nodes into exactly n groups, and the placement of one instance of the task in each of those groups. These annotations form the basic building blocks for constructing hierarchical structures in the sensor network, where the task instantiated in a certain group of nodes or geographical area acts as the cluster-head for that area.

In the current version of the ATaG compiler, this partitioning and allocation is not performed with a view to optimize any performance metric. For example, the result of compiling the annotation "nodes-per-instance:/4" will be the division of the set of sensor nodes into four groups, and the assignment of one instance of the abstract task to each group. The choice of node within each group is random. In a real-world scenario, this choice could be influenced by performance considerations. Consider a network of a hundred nodes numbered 0 through 99. For the above annotation, instantiating the associated abstract task on nodes 0, 1, 2, and 3 is correct because each of these nodes can be imagined to be representative of a group of 25 nodes that form a partition. However, if the role of this task is to collect and process data from the other 24 nodes in its group, then the geographic placement of the four nodes will greatly impact the communication costs and hence the energy performance and lifetime of the system. Ongoing work in the ATaG project is focusing on developing an efficient compiler for ATaG that takes into consideration a specific performance metric while translating annotations for a particular network deployment.

Generalizing task annotations: Attribute-based task placement. The specific annotations listed in Table 2.1 provide control over placement based on geographic location or node identifiers. While this is a useful set of annotations to define many commonly encountered patterns in sensor networking (as will be illustrated through programming idioms in Section 2.5), other useful annotations can be defined.

Consider the placement of tasks predicated on the resources available at a node in a heterogeneous networked sensor system where a sensor node could range from the Berkeley Motes to a desktop PC equipped with a webcam. For example, the programmer might wish to designate a task for placement only on sensor nodes that are equipped with an acoustic sensor. Presumably, this task will contain code that samples the acoustic sensor. Other tasks could be earmarked for sensor nodes that have the minimum computation resources, communication bandwidth, or storage (memory) capacity to support their execution. The ability to associate the requisite sensing and computation requirements of a task with its declaration is especially important for architecture-independent programming for a heterogeneous system. Note that such resource annotations can also be combined with other annotations to control, say, the placement of tasks with a specific sensing interface in a particular geographic region.

Resource annotations can also be defined for resources that are expected to change at runtime. Energy level at a node is a classic example of such a resource. An abstract task can be annotated with a particular minimum energy level so as to be invoked only when the energy resources at the node are above that limit and other invocation triggers (firing rules) are satisfied. The application of such annotation is twofold. First, it allows the system to switch between different versions of the application at runtime based on energy levels, where each version could correspond to a different pattern of computation and communication in the network. Second, it allows a node to switch from using one implementation of a task to another when the energy level drops below some threshold. From the ATaG program's perspective, this means that different subsets of the abstract tasks (and hence the associated channels and data items) in the same program are activated at different times, based on the resource availability in the network. The program therefore represents the union of possible spatio-temporal execution patterns, depending on resource availability.

The variety of task annotations defined above lead naturally to a common framework of attribute-based task placement. In the previous discussions, we have defined various categories for task annotations such as fine-grained control, density-based instantiation, resource-linked instantiation, etc. For each of these categories, we discussed representative annotations and the applicable scenarios of usage. Instead of extending the set of annotations in each categories and/or defining new categories of annotations, a common framework can be adopted based on the observation that geographic location, node identifiers, sensing interface, resource availability, etc., all characterize the state of a node at a given point in time and space. Each of these categories can be considered as a type of attribute value that a sensor node has to satisfy in order to be eligible for hosting the task. If node attributes (such as geographic location, node ID, and type of sensing interface) are known at design time and are unchanging for the target deployment, task placement can also be determined at compile time. The runtime system does not need to incorporate

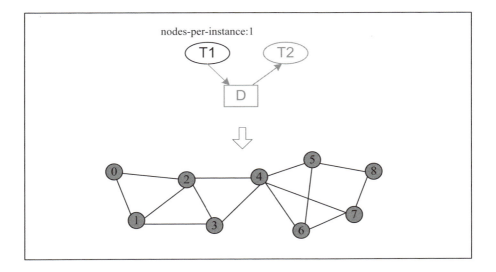

Figure 2.3   Instantiating an abstract task on each node in the network.

mechanisms to track possible changes in these attributes, thereby reducing the complexity of the runtime system software.

For other attributes such as energy level of the node, compile time decisions cannot be made because it is an inherently dynamic property of the node. In such cases, code placement can occur at compile time on all nodes of the network, while task placement is left to the runtime system. A resource management module on each node is then expected to track the corresponding attribute (in this case, the energy level) and change the task placement for that node based on the intent of the programmer.

2.3.3   Illustrative examples

In this section, we provide simple examples to help the reader visualize the effect of using a few of the task placement annotations and channel annotations to set up a variety of patterns of collaborative computation in the network. For sake of simplicity, we focus on a single abstract task and a single output channel.

Figure 2.3 shows how to instantiate an abstract task on every single node of the network by using the `nodes-per-instance` task placement annotation with the parameter 1. This is a simple but commonly occurring pattern for many environment monitoring applications, where sampler tasks on each sensor node perform periodic sampling and filtering of sensor values before further computation on them can take place.

Figure 2.4 shows the result of instantiating a task with a density of one per three nodes. Figure 2.5 shows a similar density-based instantiation that is defined in terms of area and not in terms of the sensor nodes. Each cell of the grid in the figure denotes one square meter. Although we do not show an example application that uses this type of density-based instantiation in this book, this annotation can be used in conjunction with the k-nearest-pc: 1 channel annotation to create a dynamic, hierarchical data collection pattern in the application.

The use of nodes-per-instance:/k and area-per-instance:/k to partition the network into virtual domains in terms of nodes and area, respectively, is shown in Figure 2.6 and Figure 2.7, respectively. The dashed circles in the figures show the grouping of tasks into domains that are implicitly created by the use of these annotations. The exact partitioning of the area of deployment or the set of nodes into domains is up to the compiler, and various algorithms can be applied at this state to optimize performance metrics such as energy balance and network lifetime. In the current implementation, no optimization is performed.

These annotations can be used to create tree structures with a fixed number of levels and a fixed number of nodes at each level. ATaG currently has no mechanism that will allow the creation of a flexible number of levels. For instance, consider an application with a hierarchical data collection pattern where the programmer wants four leaf (level 0) nodes to report to each level 1 node, four level 1 nodes to report to each level 2 node, and so on. Now, if the number of children of each internal node are fixed (in this case, four), then the number of levels in the tree will depend on the total number of nodes in the network. ATaG does not currently support the specification of such variable structures. The patterns shown in Figures 2.6 and 2.7 can be used to create tree structures with a fixed number of levels.

Figure 2.8 and Figure 2.9 illustrate a combination of task placement annotations and channel annotations to achieve different patterns of data dissemination. Although these examples are very simple, they form powerful building blocks in combination with other annotations listed in Tables 2.1 and 2.2. The case study in Chapter 5 will demonstrate the use of such building blocks to develop and deploy example "real-world" applications for sensor networks. Figure 2.8 shows the result of compiling the depicted ATaG program for the 9-node sensor network Task T1 is mapped onto node 4 and transmits data items

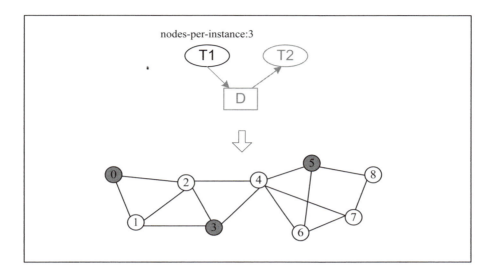

Figure 2.4   Instantiating one instance of task T1 per three sensor nodes.

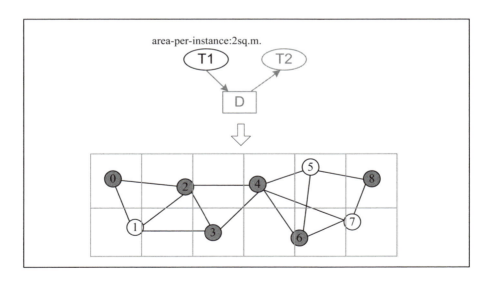

Figure 2.5   Instantiating task T1 with a density of one task per 2 square meters.

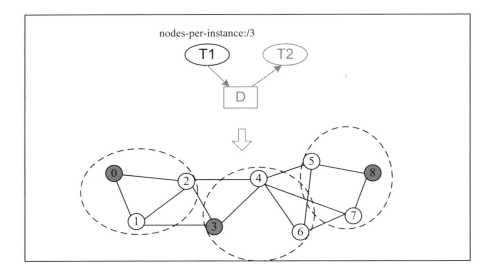

Figure 2.6 Partitioning the sensor nodes into three "equal" sets and assigning one instance of task T1 per set.

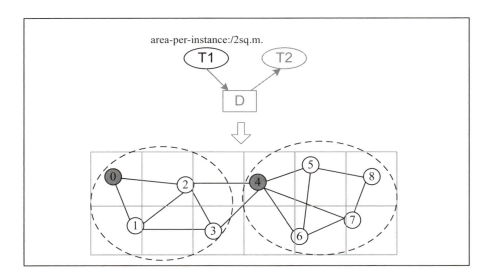

Figure 2.7 Partitioning the area of deployment into two "equal" regions and assigning one instance of task T1 per region.

to its 1-hop neighbors. The neighborhood maintenance and the mechanism for disseminating the instance of data item D to the five neighboring nodes is implemented in the runtime system. If the placement annotation for T1 is changed to `nodes-per-instance:1`, it results in the neighbor-to-neighbor interaction pattern that is used in applications such as contour detection.

Mapping an abstract task to a specific node (in this case, node 4) and transmitting a data item to its k nearest nodes shown in Figure 2.9. Consider an application where node 4 represents a handheld device that is used by a supervisor to move around the area of deployment, use a sensor interface to take readings at various points in the network, and send the information back to the supervisor station for logging. Specifying this behavior is extremely simple in the ATaG model using a pattern similar to the one shown in the figure. Suppose the data item D indicates the reading that is to be sent to the supervisor node, task T1 is the task hosted on the handheld device that performs the sampling when desired by the user, and task T2 is mapped onto the supervisor node (say node 8) and logs the readings when received. To accomplish the desired functionality, the following steps are required:

- Annotate the output channel between task T1 and data item D as `k-nearest-nodes:1`

- Annotate the input channel between data item D and task T2 as `all-nodes`

- Annotate task T2 with the `any-data` firing rule and `one-on-node-ID:8` placement annotation.

Whenever the task T1 is fired and produces data item D, it will be sent by the runtime to its nearest node in the network and then routed to the supervisor node. This example illustrates how sophisticated behaviors can be modeled using the basic set of annotations. Naturally, support for interpreting the annotations must exist in the compiler and in the runtime system.

Figure 2.10 illustrates the effect of using the `domain` channel annotation in conjunction with the partitioning annotations for task placement. Note that the domain abstraction is valid only if the task associated with the channel has a placement annotations `nodes-per-instance:/k` or `area-per-instance:/k`. As mentioned earlier, the partitioning of the set of nodes or the area of deployment is left to the compiler. The use of `domain` as the channel annotation in this case means that the scope of the dissemination (collection) of the output (input) data for an instance of the associated abstract task is defined by the partition that is 'assigned' to that task by the compiler. If the network is

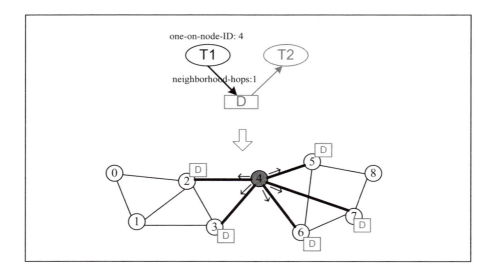

Figure 2.8   Using a combination of placement and channel annotations to disseminate data D to the 1-hop neighbors of node 4.

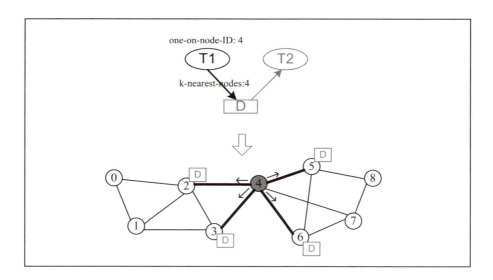

Figure 2.9   Disseminating data item D to the four nearest neighbors of node 4.

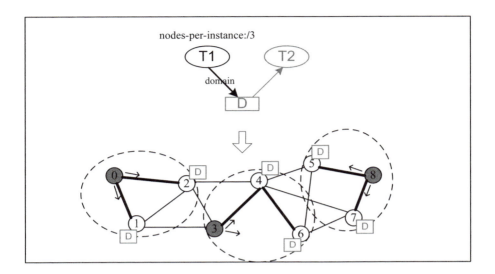

Figure 2.10   Hierarchical data dissemination among three disjoint sets of sensor nodes.

dynamic, the burden of maintaining the definition of and connectivity within the domains is entirely up to the runtime system. The end user does not worry about the low-level mechanisms involved in constructing and maintaining a domain.

2.4 SEMANTICS

2.4.1 Terminology

The following terminology is used in the remainder of this section.

- *Task*: A "task" may refer to a particular instance of an abstract task or the abstract task itself. For example, a "periodic task" means that the corresponding abstract task in the ATaG has a "periodic" firing rule. On the other hand, a "periodic task that is ready for execution" refers to a particular instance of that abstract task on some node whose firing condition has been met. Although the usage is overloaded, the meaning should be apparent from the context of its usage, especially in light of the fact that an instance of an abstract task is the executable entity, and not the abstract task itself.

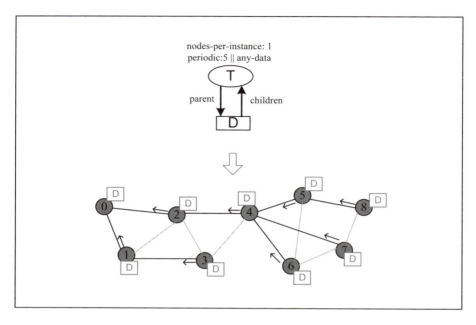

Figure 2.11   Using parent–child channel annotation to form a logical tree in the network deployment. Data are collected from child nodes and forwarded to parent nodes. In this example, the runtime system creates and maintains the tree without programmer intervention or control.

- *Data item*: The phrase "data item" always refers to an abstract data item. If an instance of a particular data item is being referred to, it will be explicitly stated.

- *Input (output) data item*: In the context of a particular abstract task, a data item is called an input (output) data item if there is an input (output) channel that associates the data item with that particular task.

- *Dependent task*: In the context of a particular data item, an abstract task is called a dependent task if there is an input channel associating the data item with that particular task.

2.4.2   Firing rules

The following rules determine when a task is considered to be ready for execution. The actual time of execution of a ready task depends on factors such as the number of tasks that might precede this task in the scheduler's queue,

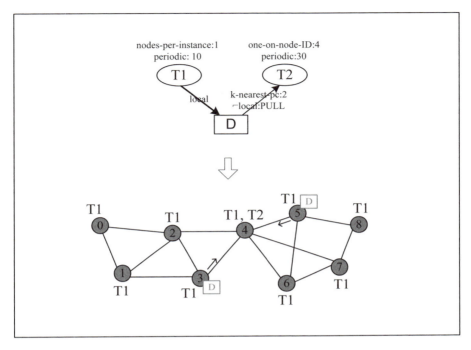

Figure 2.12   Use of the k-nearest producer annotation to dynamically collect data from the vicinity of the consumer. This annotation, with the underlying runtime support, is likely to be most useful when the consumer node is mobile and the objective of the application is to gather information from sensor nodes that lie close to the path of the consumer at any given time.

the time remaining for the currently running task to complete execution, the duration of each of the preceding tasks, etc.

- A *periodic* task is ready when the periodic timer expires, regardless of the state of its input data items. The per-task timer is set to zero each time the task begins execution and is said to expire when the timer value becomes equal to the task's period.

- An *any-data* task is ready as soon as a new instance of any of its input data items is available.

- An *all-data* task is ready as soon as a new instance of each of its input data items is available.

- A *periodic* ∨ *any-data* task is ready when the periodic timer expires or a new instance of any of the input data items is available.

- A *periodic* ∨ *all-data* is ready when the periodic timer expires or a new instance of each of the input data items is available.

- If a task is *any-data* ∨ *all-data*, the any-data firing rules apply.

2.4.3   Task graph execution

- Task execution is atomic. Each instance of an abstract task will run to completion before an instance of any other abstract task can commence execution.

- All members of the set of dependent tasks of a particular data item are executed before other tasks that might be dependent on the data items output by the tasks in this set.

- When the production of an instance of a data item results in one or more of its dependent tasks becoming ready, those tasks will consume the same instance when they invoke a get() on the input data item. This means that that particular instance that triggered the task will not be overwritten or removed from the data pool before every scheduled dependent task finishes execution.

2.4.4   get() **and** put()

A task reads its input data instances from the datapool using the get() primitive invoked as:

```
d = get(int dataID);
```

where dataID is the unique integer identifier of the desired data item.

Each invocation of the instance of a well-behaved abstract task results in exactly one invocation of get() for each of its input data items. get() is a nonblocking call in the sense that the calling task is not suspended until an instance of the requested data item becomes available. The following rules apply to the get() primitive:

- When an any-data task executes, at least one of its get() calls will succeed.

- When an all-data task executes, each of its get() calls will succeed.

- get() is a destructive read from the task's perspective. Once a particular instance of a data item is read by a task, it is considered to be eliminated from the data pool as far as that task is concerned. Subsequent calls to get() for the same data item in later invocations of the task will fail if no newer instance is available, or will return a new instance if one has been produced since the last invocation.

A task adds its output data items to the data pool by using the put() primitive invoked as:

```
boolean status = put(d);
```

where d is an instance of some data item, and status is the boolean indication of success or failure of the call.

put() is not guaranteed to succeed. This is because the ATaG runtime allows for at most one instance of each data item to be present in the data pool at a given node. If a new instance of a particular data item is produced at a node, the old instance (if any) must be overwritten, which is possible only if none of the tasks that are scheduled for execution on that node are dependent on it. If there is at least one task scheduled for execution that is dependent on the particular instance, a put() on that node will return with an indication of failure. Otherwise, the instance will be added to the node's data pool and put() will return success. The different valid states of a data item and the structure of the data pool on the node is discussed in the next subsection. The responsibility of determining the success of put() and taking appropriate action(s) at the application level is entirely the programmers'. A common scenario where put() might fail is if a periodic task is producing one or more data items at a faster rate than they can be consumed by the set of dependent tasks. The impact on the application will depend on the semantics of the data item being produced.

2.5 PROGRAMMING IDIOMS

In this section, we qualitatively demonstrate the key features of ATaG by providing sample programs for commonly encountered patterns of information flow that form the building blocks of a large class of applications. The purpose of these examples is to specifically highlight the following:

- *The ATaG data-driven model is a natural fit for specifying reactive applications.* The concepts of abstract tasks, data items, and channels concisely capture a variety of task placements, along with data dissemination and collection patterns. ATaG allows the coding of symmetric behaviors (e.g., neighbor-to-neighbor protocols), asymmetric behaviors (e.g., many-to-one data collection), and combinations of the two (e.g., local neighbor interaction resulting in an alarm condition that is then routed to a root node).

- *ATaG programs are architecture-independent.* The set of task and channel annotations allow the programmer to control the degree of architecture independence of the specification. Tasks can be placed on specific node IDs or geographic locations or the placement can be left entirely to the compilation framework. Realistic applications can be expected to employ a compromise between the two extremes, with some tasks assigned to specific nodes or locations that are known *a priori*, while others can be more flexibly mapped.

- *ATaG programming only requires familiarity with a traditional programming language such as C or Java.* The declarative part of the ATaG program (depicted by the figures accompanying each example) is specified visually. The imperative part is in a traditional sequential programming language. ATaG programming does not require the mastery of a new syntax or any extensions to traditional programming languages.

Table 2.3 Event-Reaction Pairs for Object Tracking

Event	Reaction	Scope
Periodic timer expires	Acoustic sensor is sampled	Local
Sensor reading exceeds threshold (object in range)	Propagate location- and time-stamped reading	All other nodes that may have detected the same target
Sensor reading arrives at node	Determine if own reading is higher than readings from neighbors	Local
Node elects itself the leader	Send target location to designated root node	-

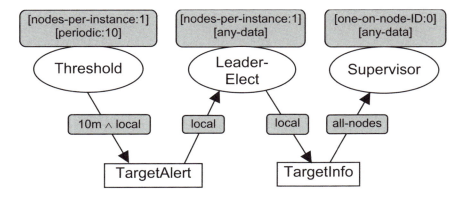

Figure 2.13   Object tracking.

2.5.1   Object tracking

Object tracking basically involves determining the location of an object in the area being monitored. A simple algorithm for object tracking [55] requires each node to periodically sample its sensing interface and compare it against a predefined threshold. A reading that exceeds the threshold is indicative of the presence of a target in the sensing range. The nodes that detect the target elect a leader node, which is the node with the maximum reading among all nodes involved in the election. The leader node then performs some processing of the set of sensor readings and transmits the resultant estimate of target location to a base station.

Figure 2.13 is a complete ATaG program for this application behavior. A prototype implementation of this application required approximately 100 lines of Java code overall. Threshold performs the sampling and thresholding on each node of the network. If a target is detected, it generates a TargetAlert data item which also carries information about the sensor reading. The assumption in this case is that the sensing range is less than half the dissemination range of 10 m, which ensures that every node that detects the target communicates its reading to every other node that has detected the target. The Leader-Elect task also runs on each node and receives the TargetAlert notifications from all nodes that have detected the target. Since Threshold is pushing the data item to a 10 m radius, the Leader-Elect task can just read from its local datapool and does not need to explicitly pull instances of data items from its neighborhood. After a requisite number of sensor readings

Table 2.4   Event-Reaction Pairs for Neighbor-to-Neighbor Protocol

Event	Reaction	Scope
Periodic timer expires	Read temperature from sensor	Local
Temperature reading available	Propagate to 1-hop neighbors	-
Temperature received from neighbor	Compare with own reading	Local

are obtained, `Leader-Elect` generates the `TargetInfo` data item if its local reading is the maximum of the readings received from other nodes.

2.5.2   Interaction within local neighborhoods

Figure 2.14 is a complete ATaG program based on neighbor-to-neighbor inter-action, which is a common technique to implement collaborative computation where the processing at a given node is a function of its own state or the state of the immediate neighbors. The technique is common because such proto-cols require a fixed, typically low amount of resources, and they scale well with network size. The purpose of this program is to periodically compare its own temperature reading with that of its 1-hop neighbors. This comparison could be used for corroboration or calibration, or to detect unusual conditions such as a fire. Only a single abstract task and a single abstract data item is sufficient to capture this behavior, as shown in the figure. The output channel is annotated with a "¬local" because an output to the local data pool of the same type of data item that is also an input may cause an infinite loop and unpredictable system behavior, depending on the scheduling policies in the runtime system.

2.5.3   In-network aggregation

Fig. 2.16 is a complete ATaG program that sets up a data aggregation tree across the network. Such a mechanism is commonly used in the computation of system-wide properties such as the minimum or maximum reading in the entire system [64].

Note that although the program indicates a virtual topology (tree), it does not specify how the tree is to be constructed or maintained. The runtime system that supports the "parent" and "children" annotations is expected to manage the required protocols. Each node of the tree applies an aggregation function

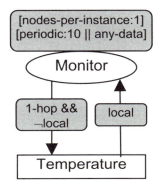

Figure 2.14   Neighbor-to-neighbor gradient monitoring.

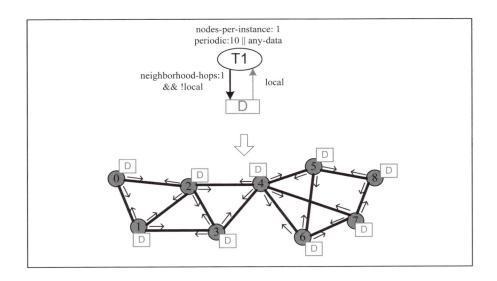

Figure 2.15   Mapping and communication: Neighbor-to-neighbor protocol.

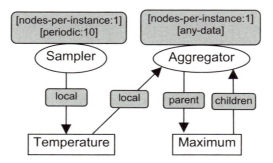

Figure 2.16 Tree-based aggregation.

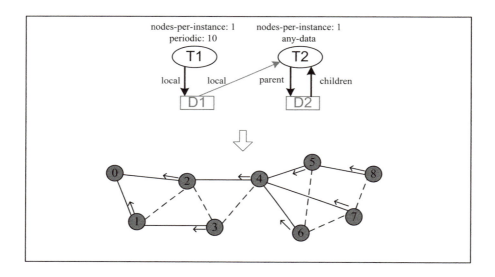

Figure 2.17 Mapping and communication: Tree-based data aggregation.

to its own periodic reading (`Sampler` task) and the readings received from its child nodes. The result is then communicated up the tree to be incrementally aggregated. This is a continuous process, driven by the periodic sampling at each node. To reduce network traffic and save energy, the Aggregator could use static variables to maintain a count of incoming packets (local state) and communicate the reading up the tree only after a certain number of invocations.

Table 2.5   Event-Reaction Pairs for Tree-Based Aggregation.

Event	Reaction	Scope
Periodic timer expires	Temperature sensor is sampled	Local
Temperature reading available from own node or other nodes	Apply aggregation function (say, MAX)	Local
Predetermined number of applications of aggregation function completed	Send aggregated reading to parent node	-

2.5.4   Hierarchical data fusion

The data aggregation tree in the previous example is a useful but simple structure. More sophisticated applications can be efficiently programmed using hierarchical data fusion. In this pattern, the network is partitioned into domains, and each domain reports to its leader. The leaders in turn are successively organized into a hierarchy with a root node at the top. A quad tree is an example of such hierarchy, with applications in topographic querying of sensor fields [7].

Figure 2.18 is a complete ATaG program that sets up a two-level quad-tree. The network is divided into four domains, each managed by one instance of the L1Fusion task. Leaf tasks report to the appropriate L1Fusion task. The Root collects the data from L1Fusion tasks. The data items are labeled LeafMap and L1Map motivated by the application discussed in [7]. The meaning of the domain annotation and the use of "/4" as a parameter for nodes-per-instance are explained in Tables 2.2 and 2.1 respectively.

Table 2.6   Event-Reaction Pairs for Hierarchical Data Fusion.

Event	Reaction	Scope
Periodic timer expires on leaf node	Temperature reading sampled	Local
Temperature reading available at leaf node	Reading sent to parent	-
Reading received at L1 clusterhead	Apply aggregation function	Local
Predetermined number of readings received at clusterhead	Send result of aggregation to root node	-

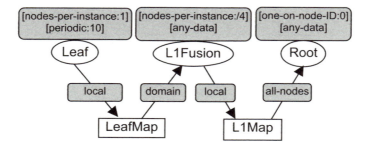

Figure 2.18 Hierarchical data fusion.

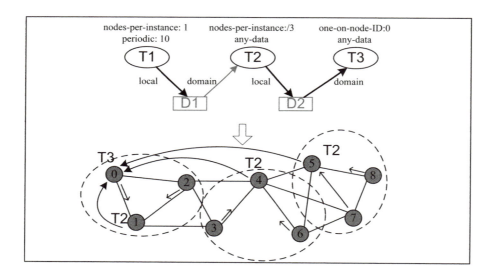

Figure 2.19 Mapping and communication: Hierarchical data fusion.

2.5.5 Event-triggered behavior instantiation

The set of collaborative behaviors used to compose distributed spatial computing applications is usually known at design time. However, it is not desirable from both a performance and functionality point of view to execute all behaviors at all times. Especially in systems that monitor and respond to events in the physical environment, there could be quiescent behaviors that are built into

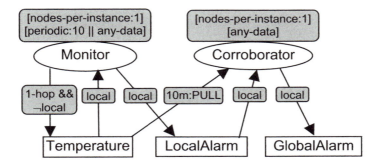

Figure 2.20   Wide-area data collection triggered by a local alarm.

the system at design time, but are to be instantiated only when certain conditions are satisifed at runtime. The conditions could denote a variety of events such as resource depletion at a critical node, abnormal sensor readings, etc.

Table 2.7   Event-Reaction Pairs for Alarm-Triggered Data Collection.

Event	Reaction	Scope
Temperature gradient exceeds threshold	Produce alarm notification	Local
Alarm notification produced	Request temperature readings for corroboration	All nodes within a 10 m radius
Readings corroborate local alarm	Produce global alarm	Local

The previous examples used abstract data items primarily to pass information such as the sensor reading or information derived from sensor readings such as a topographic map of the sensor field. However, the semantics of ATaG also allow the instantiation of new behaviors at runtime by using abstract data items to represent the *occurrence* of events, in addition to passing *information* about the events.

Figure 2.20 is a complete ATaG program for an application that monitors temperature gradients between nodes and triggers a data collection and anomaly corroboration over a larger neighborhood if a node detects a high gradient between itself and its neighbors. Only if the anomaly is confirmed does the node produce an alarm event possibly targeted for some supervisor task. The data item LocalAlarm is used to trigger the collection of data from

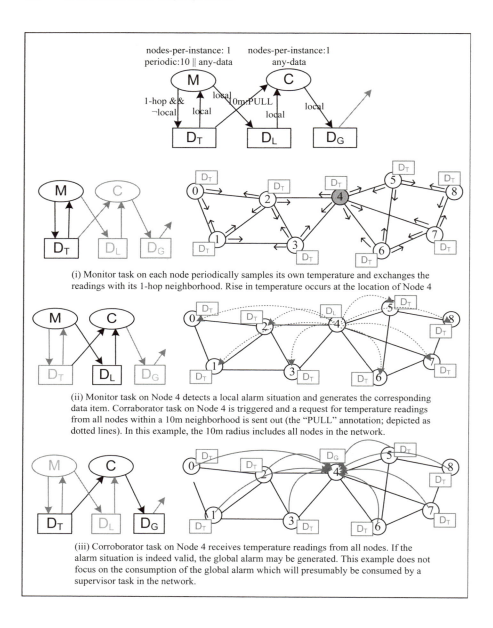

(i) Monitor task on each node periodically samples its own temperature and exchanges the readings with its 1-hop neighborhood. Rise in temperature occurs at the location of Node 4

(ii) Monitor task on Node 4 detects a local alarm situation and generates the corresponding data item. Corraborator task on Node 4 is triggered and a request for temperature readings from all nodes within a 10m neighborhood is sent out (the "PULL" annotation; depicted as dotted lines). In this example, the 10m radius includes all nodes in the network.

(iii) Corroborator task on Node 4 receives temperature readings from all nodes. If the alarm situation is indeed valid, the global alarm may be generated. This example does not focus on the consumption of the global alarm which will presumably be consumed by a supervisor task in the network.

Figure 2.21   Patterns of task execution and communication in an event-triggered data collection scenario. The abstract task graph for this example is the same as that shown in Figure 2.20, although task and data item names have been abbreviated.

nodes within a radius of 10 m. Note that the firing rule for the Corroborator task is any-data. Also, the input channel from Temperature to Corroborator has pull semantics. When the Monitor detects a discrepancy, it produces a LocalAlarm. Due to the any-data firing rule, the Corroborator is scheduled for execution, and the pull semantics then initiate a collection of data from the neighborhood. The Corroborator will use persistent storage (static variables) across instantiations to store the collected temperature readings, and it will produce a GlobalAlarm if the LocalAlarm is corroborated by neighboring nodes.

2.6 FUTURE WORK

2.6.1 State-based dynamic behaviors

The set of task and channel annotations listed and briefly described in Tables 2.1 and 2.2 are useful for describing many behaviors that form the building blocks of networked sensing applications in domains such as environment monitoring and non-real-time object tracking.[1]

What the current set of annotations really provides is an abbreviated, concise, and architecture-independent representation of task placement and coordination in an application that can be otherwise developed manually, although with a much greater effort, using a language such as nesC or C. The examples shown as programming idioms can be developed in a top-down manner by first defining the event-reaction-scope tuples and then translating them into the abstract task graph. The same ATaG program could also be developed in a bottom-up manner by inspecting the placement and communication of tasks in the desired application on a concrete network deployment and then abstracting the communication patterns as channels, the types of functionalities as abstract task with placement annotations, and the types of data exchanged as abstract data items.

A promising avenue for future work is to define high-level annotations that go beyond mere task placement and communication pathway instantiation. An example of such a class of annotations is state-based dynamic selection from among alternate implementations of the same abstract task. State could refer to a broad range of parameters such as the resource availability on a particular sensor node, density of deployment in the neighborhood of the sensor

---

[1]Since timing requirements cannot be indicated in the ATaG program and the runtime system may or may not include routing protocols that provide timing guarantees or other latency-related quality of service (QoS) requirements, we refer to the object tracking example as nonreal time.

node, the instantiation of one or more abstract tasks in a certain vicinity of the sensor node, etc. The tradeoff between quality of the result of a computation and the resources required to attain that quality—and algorithms to dynamically adjust for this tradeoff—has been an area of research in high performance scientific computing [10]. In sensor networks consisting of energy and bandwidth constrained sensor nodes, the application developer might wish to exercise control over the amount of resources that are devoted to some functionality based on the value of parameters such as the state of the energy resources remaining at that node. Such control can be used to (i) optimize application-level execution by switching to a different implementation of the same task when energy levels decrease and (ii) provide graceful degradation of functionality as resources are progressively exhausted. To support such a program specification, the abstract task will now be associated with one or more implementations in the same language meant to be invoked under different circumstances at runtime. A new class of annotations will be required to allow the user to (concisely and precisely) specify the state of the node that is a trigger for a particular implementation.

Although the ability to select a different implementation of the same abstract tasks at different times on the same node enables new ways of resource management for application-level quality of service, an equally useful feature is the ability to control which implementation of the abstract task will run on a particular sensor node, depending on state information available after deployment. In the latter case, the implementation may or may not change after runtime. Note that this is different from the task placement annotations in the current model which allow the application developer to influence which abstract task is placed on which node in the network, but do not allow the selection between different implementations of abstract tasks.

The idea of state of a node—a simple example of which is the amount of energy available on that node as a fraction of the total energy at initialization time—can be generalized to represent the state of the neighborhood. For instance, consider a deployment where a designated root node wishes to receive a particular amount of data (e.g, a particular number of temperature samples per hour) from each region of the sensor network. Now, if the density of sensor nodes in a particular region is high, sampler tasks in that region could report their (aggregated) readings with a lower frequency compared to a region where the density of deployment is less.

Examples of more sophisticated annotations that will require significant enhancements both to the ATaG model as well as to the runtime system include: "Execute implementation I of task T only if it can be executed for every invocation of task T in the next 2 hours." Such annotations will bridge the gap between the end users' understanding of the application requirements and their corresponding specification in the ATaG program. The challenge in defining this particular annotation is to devise a mechanism in the runtime which is capable of predicting the resource usage on the node (with some degree of confidence) based on activity observed on that node in the past.

2.6.2 Resource management in the runtime system

Two aspects of resource management are of interest in the context of extending the ATaG model. The first deals with the efficient *management of sensing resources* and the packaging of sensing as a service provided by the runtime instead of a set of APIs to be learnt by the programmer and invoked by the application-level program. The second aspect deals with allowing the application developer to provide performance-related hints to the compiler. We now discuss each of these in more detail.

Sensing as a service. Currently, there are three classes of APIs available to the ATaG programmer: (i) the get() and put() calls to the data pool for consuming and producing data items respectively, (ii) the network-awareness and spatial-awareness API (also offered by the runtime system) that allows a task instance to determine the composition of the neighborhood of its host node, and (iii) the API to the sensor interface. Since the task instance directly accesses the sensing interface, the runtime system is not aware of the access patterns and cannot optimize for cases where sensing resources might be used inefficiently. Consider a scenario where a periodic Task A is interested in sensor data not more than 10 minutes old, and Task B is interested in the same sensor data but with a tolerance of 30 minutes. In the current model, Task A and Task B will be defined as abstract tasks with periodic firing rules with periods of 10 minutes and 30 minutes, respectively. The tasks will read from the sensor at each invocation, although it is obvious that frequency of Task A's sampling is sufficient for Task B. A manual optimization in this case is to declare an abstract data item S produced locally by Task A and consumed locally by Task B, and to change the firing rule of Task B to "any-data." Task A will now sample the sensing interface at every invocation but will produce an instance of S (containing the sensor reading) every third invocation. However, such manual optimization is not possible if Task A and Task B are part of different ATaG libraries being composed into a larger application.

Future work in this area involves the management of sensing (and actuation) resources through the ATaG runtime system. The ATaG model will be extended by defining a special class of *read-only abstract data items* (called "sensor data items") that can be consumed but not produced by user-defined abstract tasks. These data items will represent readings (scalar values, images, etc.) from the sensing interface(s). Task will access sensor data using the get() primitive, and the programmer will not be required to learn the details of accessing the variety of sensor interfaces. A set of annotations will be defined for the sensor data items. These annotations could indicate the type of sensing interface and other parameters such as spatial coverage and temporal coverage (frequency of sampling, freshness of data, etc.). This extension will allow the runtime a greater flexibility in task placement and resource management. More importantly, indirect access of sensor interfaces through the runtime system makes ATaG programs even more architecture-independent because the imperative part of the program (i.e., the task code) does not need to incorporate any code that is specific to a particular type of sensor or actuator. Nodes with diffent sensors of the same type (i.e., producing the same type of sensor data item) can host instances of the same abstract task without the programmer being required to modify the code to adjust for the different sensor APIs.

Application-level control of system performance. In almost all traditional parallel and distributed computing especially in scientific computing, all data were equal. The scheduling of tasks and handling of data was almost entirely influenced by end-to-end latency considerations. Hence, the many variants of the basic task graph (or other dependency graphs) did not support the concept of varying levels of "importance" that could be assigned to tasks or data. The nature of networked sensing is such that some data items and computation pathways could have greater importance than others, where importance could imply preferential processing in terms of immediate scheduling of the tasks involved or allocating more resources to ensure that some data items are routed with better "quality" (e.g., less latency) than others. For example, if the instance of the abstract data item represents the (possible) detection of a forest fire, the application developer would naturally want the runtime system to expedite the transmission of this data from the producer node to the designated supervisor node. Defining and supporting such annotations also requires a close integration with the network model, the architecture of the runtime system, and the availability of protocols that are capable of providing the required services.

2.6.3   Utility-based negotiation for task scheduling and resource allocation

Service-oriented specification of networked sensing applications is a vision where programming for sensor networks essentially involves the specification of semantic information desired by the end user. This purely declarative high-level specification is used to first select a set of services from the library of available services for the target network, where each "service" could map to an independent application with a well-defined interface for integration with other applications. In the context of ATaG where composition of two independent ATaG program is equivalent—in the simplest case where the two programs do not share data or functionality—to the concatenation of the corresponding task graphs, each service could naturally map to an ATaG program. Of course, this requires a new markup language for describing ATaG programs in terms of the services they provide to the end user, similar to semantic streams [57].

Assuming that the component subprograms can be identified from the high-level specification and that the final mapping of tasks to nodes and the setup of communication pathways in the network is accomplished, the next problem is to manage resource allocation in face of conflicting requests from application tasks. For example, two tasks on the same node could request an image from the camera at the same time, but require the camera to be pointing in different directions. A *utility-based negotiator* in the runtime could decide the resource allocation in such scenarios. The challenge is to develop a robust and scalable implementation of utility-based negotiation and to define a common utility scale that can be used across disparately developed ATaG libraries that are combined into a larger application. The concept of utility could also model task priorities and resolve conflicts when more than one task simultaneously requests preferential treatment. The key challenge in extending the basic model to handle such scenarios is to maintain the core design objectives—especially application neutrality—while enabling the expression of increasingly sophisticated behaviors.

CHAPTER 3

DART: THE DATA-DRIVEN ATAG RUNTIME

3.1 DESIGN OBJECTIVES

3.1.1 Support for ATaG semantics

The primary objective of DART is to provide the required underlying mechanisms for communication and coordination between instances of abstract tasks specified by the programmer. Architecture independence of ATaG is ensured primarily by the deployment-specific interpretation of the generic task and channel annotations. Depending on the characteristics of the underlying network, the responsibility of translating the annotations could be distributed between the compile-time code generator and the runtime system itself. For instance, consider an output channel with an annotation *neighborhood-hops:1*, indicating that the data item produced by the assocated task is to be sent to all the 1-hop neighbors of the node where the item is produced.

Architecture-Independent Programming for Wireless Sensor Networks
By Amol B. Bakshi, Viktor K. Prasanna
Copyright © 2008 John Wiley & Sons, Inc.

For a network composed of relatively resource-rich nodes such as Stargates [50] connected by a robust wireless network, this annotation can be translated at compile time. The compiler will analyze the network graph, determining the nodes that will host the associated task, determine the IDs or geographic locations of the 1-hop neighbors (depending on the routing protocol being used), and hardcode the list of destinations for that data item into the runtime system. Every time an instance of the data item is produced, the runtime system will look up the IDs of the destination set (which is, in this scenario, assumed to be unchanging) and send the data item to each member of that set.

On the other hand, the same ATaG program could be synthesized onto an underlying network that is dynamic in nature where the set of neighbors of a node is expected to change frequently: nodes being added or removed from the network (in a mobile setting), nodes failing due to exhaustion of limited energy resources, unreliable communication due to the hostile environment, etc. Clearly, the compile time analysis of the network graph is not feasible in such a scenario, and the runtime system supports runtime translation of the *neighborhood-hops:1* annotation into the instantaneous membership of the set of 1-hop neighbors. In addition, there are decisions to be made about how frequently should the runtime system update its view of the neighborhood, the impact of such updation on the performance and of the system, etc.

3.1.2   Platform independence

The objective of the DART design is not so much on the implementation of an ATaG runtime system for a particular sensor node platform or a particular language and operating system, but on the architecture of a runtime system *template* that will hopefully be useful for implementing versions of DART tailored to specific platforms. This means that the assumptions about the underlying operating system implicit in the operation of the DART template should be clearly spelled out and should also be minimized. Specifically, assumptions about the type of scheduler, support for multi-threading, synchronization and inter-process coordination primitives, etc., should be explicitly stated. Ideally, any operating system kernel that provides these basic facilities should be a friendly target for implementing DART.

Such platform independence is important because an important purpose of the ATaG programming model is to hide almost all the low-level details of control and coordination from the programmer, allowing him/her to focus only on expressing the desired behavior in terms of data-driven event–reaction semantics with suitable annotations to govern deployment-specific task placement and communication. This architecture independence makes ATaG a good candidate for implementation on heterogeneous system architectures. Unless the architecture of the underlying runtime system is defined in a platform-independent manner, a "seamless" deployment of ATaG on such systems will not be possible.

3.1.3   Component-based design

Components are "units of independent production, acquisition, and deployment that interact to form a functioning system" [51]. A component is the deployment of one or more interfaces that define the service offered by the component to its consumers. Since the customers rarely care about how the particular interface is implemented, the data and algorithms used internally by the component (module) implementation can be considered to be "owned" by the module and the implementation details will typically be hidden from other modules. This also means that development of a component is decoupled from its integration into the system. Indeed, a variety of implementations of the same component (i.e., providing the same service by implementing the same interface(s)) can be developed to meet various requirements, and the suitable implementation can be selected at the time of composition.

The modular structure of component-based design has many significant advantages. First, it greatly simplifies the design by requiring the clear identification of components in terms of what exactly they model in the problem domain. Interactions and dependencies between components are also defined in terms of service provider and service consumer relationships. Second, as mentioned above, hiding the implementation of a module from other modules makes it possible for an entirely different set of protocols to be used to provide the same service interface without affect the rest of the system. In the specific case of the ATaG, this allows the runtime system to be tailored for a specific target platform by selecting the suitable intra-module protocols without requiring a complete redesign.

For instance, one of the modules of DART is responsible for translating channel annotations into list of node IDs or locations. The list of channel annotations used by the ATaG program is known at compile time. This knowledge can be used by the software synthesis process to include only those protocols in this module as are required to translate all the annotations actually used in the program and not all the annotations supported in the ATaG model. For example, an application may not require a virtual topology (such as a tree) and therefore may not employ the *parent* and *children* annotations in the ATaG program. When this application is synthesized, the ability to translate *parent* and *children* annotations is not required in the runtime and the protocol to construct and maintain a logical tree is also not included in the synthesized software. Indeed, the runtime system can be customized differently for each node, based on the services (protocols) required by the tasks instantiated on that node. Component design of the ATaG runtime system can also be seen as a step toward defining **standards** to be followed by the designers of a particular protocol for, say, routing, to ensure that the result is usable in a "real" end-to-end system.

Another side effect of this design is that it allowed us to use essentially the same runtime system software for functional simulation as is intended for real deployments, by replacing only a subset of the modules—especially those that deal with the transceiver interface—and leaving others intact.

3.1.4   Ease of software synthesis

We have built an end-to-end application development framework based on the ATaG programming model that also includes a tool for synthesis of compile-ready customized software for the individual node of the target network, based on the ATaG program and the network description. The synthesized software for a node has three components: (i) a common DART kernel that runs on every node and handles basic tasks such as data pool management, managing the basic networking protocols, etc., (ii) user-supplied code for abstract tasks and user-supplied data structures (and methods) for abstract data items, and (iii) glue code for the interface between the runtime and the user-supplied code.

The user-supplied code and the common runtime code are available to the software synthesizer, and ease of software synthesis can be measured by the size of the glue code that is to be generated for a particular node for a particular ATaG program. The choice of data-driven computing as the programming paradigm for ATaG is also influenced by the fact that in a data-driven software system, the only interaction between the user-supplied code and the runtime system is through the get() and put() calls implemented in the datapool manager. Therefore, the purpose of the glue code that is to be synthesized can be broadly classified as follows:

- *Allowing the runtime to interact with application tasks*, i.e., to determine their attributes (such as firing rule and input–output interface), schedule the tasks for execution through suitable interfaces such as the Runnable interface of Java if the application tasks are provided as Java classes implementing Runnable, etc.

- *Providing state information (context awareness)* required by the node to situate itself in the network. For instance, if nodes have preassigned identifiers, the ID should be hardcoded into and accessible through a suitable function call by the modules of the runtime system. For scenarios where the program is synthesized onto relatively static and robust networks (as discussed above in Section 3.1.1), information such as the composition of the node's neighborhood will be incorporated into the runtime system at software synthesis time. Other information such as the role of the node in a virtual topology (if any) will also be determined and incorporated into the software. For instance, on initialization after deployment, each node will check if it is supposed to be the designated root node and, based on the (boolean) result of the query, adjust the behavior of its protocols for virtual topology formation.

- *Pre-wiring communication pathways.* Consider a simple ATaG program for centralized data collection with two abstract tasks and one abstract data item. The programmer uses channel annotations to indicate that all data produced by the Sampler on each node is to be routed to the Collector on some designated root node. The placement of the Collector is specified by the annotation of that abstract task—say, as the node with ID 0. When a data item is produced on some non-root node, the runtime system on that node should know the destination of the data, i.e., the location or ID of the root node. In some deployments, the ID and location of the designated root node could be fixed and known *a priori* (e.g., it might be a gateway node connected to the desktop PC of the building supervisor). In such cases, the runtime systems on non-root node can be preprogrammed with a destination list (in this case, the root node) for the data item in question. Scenarios where this might not be suitable are when the root node itself is dynamic (say, a PDA device carried by the building supervisor) or the selection of a node as the root is performed only after the system is initialized.

3.2 OVERVIEW

Figure 3.1 is a high-level overview of the structure of DART (**D**ata-driven **A**TaG **R**un**T**ime). In this section, we briefly discuss the functionalities of the various components and their interactions. Later subsections focus in detail on the implementation of each component.

The software system on each node can be divided into an application layer that consists of (a) the user-supplied code for each abstract task placed on that

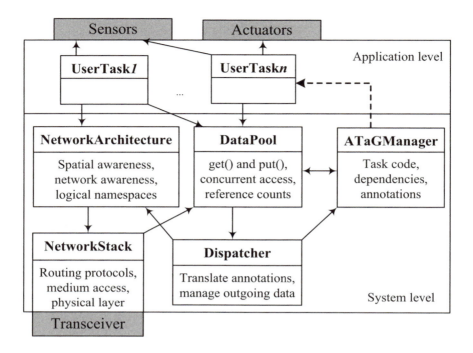

Figure 3.1   DART: The ATaG runtime system.

node and (b) a system-layer that contains the modules of the runtime system. Presently, the sensor/actuator interfaces are not managed by the runtime, although that is the subject of future work. Hence, if an abstract task requires access to the sensor or actuator interface, the necessary code has to be supplied by the programmer, who is also required to understand the APIs involved. The two-system level interfaces that are available to the user tasks are the Datapool and the NetworkArchitecture, as shown in Figure 3.1.

- The Datapool components on all nodes in the network together manage the production, consumption, localization, and routing of all instances of abstract data items produced in the network. They provide the abstraction of a single logical pool of data items that is uniformly accessed by all tasks in the system using the basic get() and put() primitives.

- The AtagManager component acts as the respository of all relevant information concerning the declarative part of the ATaG program that might be required by other components for intranode coordination and internode communication. This information includes the number of abstract tasks, data, and channels, the task and channel annotations, input–output relationships between tasks and data items on that node, and the firing rule for each task. The `AtagManager` also schedules the application-level tasks for execution when their firing conditions are met.

- `NetworkArchitecture` is the component responsible for managing all protocols for neighbor discovery, virtual topology formation, etc., with the objective of providing the mechanism to translate a channel annotation into a list of node identifiers. For instance, if a data item is to be sent to the 'parent' node in the virtual tree topology, it is the role of this component to implement the protocols for tree formation and maintenance and, when queried, return the ID of the neighboring node that is the current parent.

- As indicated by its name, the `NetworkStack` is in charge of communication with other nodes in the network and also manages the routing, medium access, and physical layer protocols.

- The `Dispatcher` is a helper component that coordinates between the `Datapool`, `AtagManager`, `NetworkArchitecture`, and `Network-Stack` with the purpose of transmitting instances of data items produced on the node to their suitable destinations in the network, as indicated by the annotations of the output channel associated with the data item in the ATaG program.

In the following sections, we describe each component of DART in more detail. To highlight the component-based design of the software system, the service offered by each component is described first, followed by the consumers of that service, and finally the implementation details of the service. Note that the primary objective of the current version of DART is to demonstrate the feasibility and usefulness of programming with ATaG. The programming and software synthesis environment (Section 4) for ATaG has an accompanying simulation and visualization front-end. The current implementation of DART is meant to be a component of this simulation environment that runs on a single machine. Although DART is designed as a component-based template for a general ATaG runtime, some of the low-level functionalities (such as routing protocols and topology formation protocols) that will be required for DART to run on a multi-node distributed sensor node deployment have been replaced by code that simulates these functionalities for single-machine simulation. As highlighted in Section 3.1.3, the advantage of component-based design is that the implementation of a component can be changed as long as the service it provides remains the same. Hence, the replacement of some of the functionalities within a component by functionally equivalent code that simulates their existence could be performed without affecting other components such as `Datapool`, `AtagManager`, `Dispatcher`, etc.

3.3   COMPONENTS AND FUNCTIONALITIES

3.3.1   Task, data, and channel declarations

The declarative content of an ATaG program is stored in the runtime as instances of the `TaskDeclaration` and `ChannelDeclaration` classes. We do not define a data declaration class because no annotations are currently associated with the data items.

A UML class diagram of the `TaskDeclaration` class is shown in Figure 3.2. Code listings showing the variables and the `runTask()` method of this class are provided as Figures 3.3 and fig:td-runtask, respectively.

The task declaration stores the firing rule and instantiation (placement) annotations for that task. A pointer to the actual task code (a Java class that supports the `Runnable` interface) is also stored. Pointers to input and output channels associated with the task are stored as arrays with a '1' in entry k of the input (output) array signifying that the input (output) channel with ID k is associated with that task.

In addition, a boolean variable `hasBeenRun` is defined, with an initial value of `false`. This variable is necessary due to the way periodic task execution is handled in the current DART implementation. An application-level (user-defined) task is just a Java class that supports the `Runnable` interface and interacts with the `DataPool` and possibly the `NetworkArchitecture` modules through appropriate function calls. If a task is to be run periodically, say, with a period of 5 minutes, then the delay loop is included (and automatically generated) in that task itself. Specifically, the task runs in a permanent "while(1)" loop with a 5-minute delay as the last statement of the loop.

At startup, all periodic tasks that are assigned to the node are launched, and their `hasBeenRun` flag is set to true to indicate this fact. During the course of application execution, when a data item is produced, its dependent tasks are to be scheduled for execution. The `AtagManager` calls the `runTask()` routine for the corresponding task declarations. The `hasBeenRun` flag ensures that if

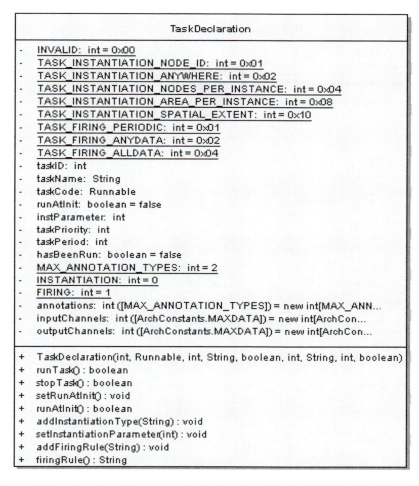

TaskDeclaration
- INVALID: int = 0x00
- TASK_INSTANTIATION_NODE_ID: int = 0x01
- TASK_INSTANTIATION_ANYWHERE: int = 0x02
- TASK_INSTANTIATION_NODES_PER_INSTANCE: int = 0x04
- TASK_INSTANTIATION_AREA_PER_INSTANCE: int = 0x08
- TASK_INSTANTIATION_SPATIAL_EXTENT: int = 0x10
- TASK_FIRING_PERIODIC: int = 0x01
- TASK_FIRING_ANYDATA: int = 0x02
- TASK_FIRING_ALLDATA: int = 0x04
- taskID: int
- taskName: String
- taskCode: Runnable
- runAtInit: boolean = false
- instParameter: int
- taskPriority: int
- taskPeriod: int
- hasBeenRun: boolean = false
- MAX_ANNOTATION_TYPES: int = 2
- INSTANTIATION: int = 0
- FIRING: int = 1
- annotations: int ([MAX_ANNOTATION_TYPES]) = new int[MAX_ANN...
- inputChannels: int ([ArchConstants.MAXDATA]) = new int[ArchCon...
- outputChannels: int ([ArchConstants.MAXDATA]) = new int[ArchCon...
+ TaskDeclaration(int, Runnable, int, String, boolean, int, String, int, boolean)
+ runTask() : boolean
+ stopTask() : boolean
+ setRunAtInit() : void
+ runAtInit() : boolean
+ addInstantiationType(String) : void
+ setInstantiationParameter(int) : void
+ addFiringRule(String) : void
+ firingRule() : String

Figure 3.2   Storing abstract task declarations in the TaskDeclaration class.

the task is a periodic task and has already been launched at node initialization, it is not scheduled again.

A note on managing execution of periodic tasks.   The above method of managing periodic tasks is not desirable for the following two reasons. First, leaving the control of periodicity to the while loop within the task makes the runtime system less capable of controlling the task execution or being aware of the current state of the task. In the future, we would like to support changes to the ATaG program after compilation, when the application is already running in

```
// ifdefs for annotation values
private static final int INVALID = 0x00;
private static final int TASK_INSTANTIATION_NODE_ID = 0x01;
private static final int TASK_INSTANTIATION_ANYWHERE = 0x02;
private static final int TASK_INSTANTIATION_NODES_PER_INSTANCE = 0x04;
private static final int TASK_INSTANTIATION_AREA_PER_INSTANCE = 0x08;
private static final int TASK_INSTANTIATION_SPATIAL_EXTENT = 0x10;

private static final int TASK_FIRING_PERIODIC = 0x01;
private static final int TASK_FIRING_ANYDATA = 0x02;
private static final int TASK_FIRING_ALLDATA = 0x04;

// local variables
private int taskID;
private String taskName;
private Runnable taskCode;
private boolean runAtInit = false;
private int instParameter;
private int taskPriority;
private int taskPeriod;

// record if a runTask has been called on this or not.
private boolean hasBeenRun = false;

// indices into array that stores annotations
private static final int MAX_ANNOTATION_TYPES = 2;
private static final int INSTANTIATION = 0;
private static final int FIRING = 1;
private int[] annotations = new int[MAX_ANNOTATION_TYPES];

private int[] inputChannels = new int[ArchConstants.MAXDATA];
private int[] outputChannels = new int[ArchConstants.MAXDATA];
```

Figure 3.3   The internal variables of the TaskDeclaration class.

```
public boolean runTask() {
  if ( (this.firingRule().compareToIgnoreCase("periodic") == 0) &
                    this.hasBeenRun) {
    // Task is periodic.  Already scheduled to run periodically.
    return false;
  }
  else {
    // create new thread (Runnable) for this task
    Thread t_taskThread = new Thread(taskCode);
    // set specified priority for this task
    t_taskThread.setPriority(taskPriority);
    t_taskThread.start();
    // record the fact that this task has been launched
    // this is required for periodic tasks because the actual loop
    // that executes the task periodically is in the task code itself
    // and not in the runtime
    hasBeenRun = true;
    return true;
  }
}
```

Figure 3.4   The runTask() routine of the TaskDeclaration class.

the field. For instance, if a new behavior is to be added or an existing behavior is to be modified, it should not be necessary to shut down the system, reprogram each node, and reinitialize the sensor network. Instead, a protocol will be defined that can manipulate the task and channel annotations, add new tasks on a set of nodes, etc., while the system is running. Part of this manipulation could include changing the firing rule of a task from `periodic` to `any-data` or vice versa. In the current implementation, where the periodic firing rule is hard-coded in the user task class, this modification will be impossible.

Second, the semantics of the periodic firing rule are not exactly satisfied with this implementation. In ATaG, if a task is defined as periodic with, say, a 5-minute period, it means that successive invocations of the task are separated by 5 minutes. This time is measured from the start of one invocation to the start of the next invocation. If a 5-minute delay is inserted as the last statement of the while loop (as is the case currently), the specified 5 minute period applies (incorrectly) from the end of execution of the first invocation and the beginning of execution of the second. By incorporating a more sophisticated mechanism for task management in the `AtagManager`, the runtime system should ensure that the firing of the periodic timer (again, maintained by the runtime) results in a call to the `runTask()` routine of the corresponding task declaration.

The UML class diagram for the `ChannelDeclaration` class is shown in Figure 3.5. The channel declaration stores all the annotations and corresponding parameter values for the channel. The class provides methods that are used to query for the (a) type (input or output) of the channel and (b) annotation types and associated parameter values for the channel.

3.3.2 UserTask

3.3.2.1 Service Each abstract task in the ATaG model is required to be an instance of `UserTask`. The `UserTask` class is the imperative part of the abstract task declaration and contains the application-level code represented by the abstract task. From the perspective of the DART design, the service interface provided by this component is basically the Java `Runnable` interface that is invoked when this task is to be scheduled for execution.

3.3.2.2 Interactions The user-level task interacts with the `Datapool` by accessing the `get()` and `put()` functions for reading and writing data items, respectively. `UserTask` can also use the interface provided by the `NetworkArchitecture` component to obtain the list of node IDs (or locations) that constitute a specific neighborhood of the node defined either in terms of hops or Euclidean distance. For instance, the input channel for that

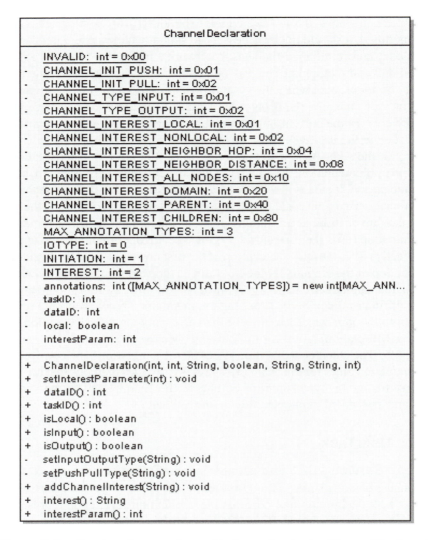

Figure 3.5   Storing abstract channel information in the ChannelDeclaration class.

user task might be annotated as *neighborhood-hops:1*, which means that each piece of incoming data is from one of the 1-hop neighbors of that node. If the functionality of the abstract task is to wait until at least one reading is received from each neighbor, and then aggregate the set of readings, it is important for the task to be able to determine how many 1-hop neighbors it has

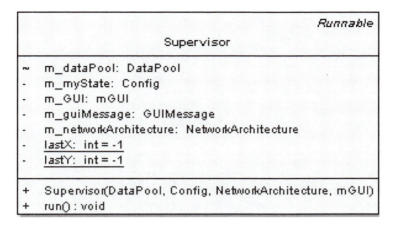

Figure 3.6   UML diagram: Supervisor (instance of UserTask).

and what their locations or IDs are, so as to be able to decide when the round of collection can be considered complete. This information is maintained by the `NetworkArchitecture` module and can optionally be accessed via the suitable query interface if required by the user task. Finally, the `UserTask` can use the APIs provided by the sensors and/or actuators on the node. In the current version of DART, sensing resources are to be accessed directly by the `UserTask` by calling the suitable methods for classes representing the sensing interfaces.

3.3.2.3 Implementation   `UserTask` is basically a Java class that implements the `Runnable` interface so that the `AtagManager` can schedule it for execution when its firing rules are deemed to be satisfied. In our programming and software synthesis framework, the code template for each instance of `UserTask` corresponding to a different abstract task is generated automatically. This template consists of the task constructor and some other attributes such as a reference to the `DataPool` that is required for invoking `get()` and `put()`, etc.

Sample ATaG code listing for the Monitor task of Figure 2.20 is shown in Figure 3.7. The ATaG programmer will write a similar piece of code for each abstract task. Note that the program is written in a traditional language (Java in this case) and involves only the manipulation of data items that correspond to application-level events. No calls to the networking stack or any other system level services are explicitly invoked. The code also does not involve any calls to other application-level tasks – a characteristic of data-driven program flow.

```
public class Monitor extends UserTask {
  // local variables to maintain state
  private static int myReading = 0;
  private static boolean wasAlarm = false, isAlarm = false;
  private static int[] targetReadings;
  [...]

  public Monitor(DataPool dp, Config myconfig,
         NetworkArchitecture t_networkArchitecture, mGUI t_GUI){
    super(dp, myconfig, t_networkArchitecture, t_GUI);
    // obtain information about the neighborhood of interest
    neighborIDs = m_networkArchitecture.kHopNeighborIDs(1);
    neighborCoords = m_networkArchitecture.kHopNeighborCoords(1);
    [...]
  }

  public void run() {
    DataItem t_dataItem = m_dataPool.getData(
            IDConstants.T_MONITOR, IDConstants.D_TEMPERATURE);
    [...]
      m_temperature = (Temperature) t_dataItem.core();
      // store the received temperature reading with its origin
      if (t_dataItem.originID() == m_myState.myID())
        myReading = m_temperature.get();
      else
        setNeighborReading(senderID, m_temperature.get());

      // check if gradient is exceeded
      for (int n=0; n<neighborIDs.length; n++) {
        if (Math.abs(getNeighborReading(n) - myReading) > 5) {
          isAlarm = true;
          break;
        }
      }
      // alarm produced only at transition (alarm to no-alarm)
      if (isAlarm && !wasAlarm) { // no-alarm->alarm transition
        wasAlarm = isAlarm;
        m_lAlarm = new LocalAlarm();
        DataItem m_dataitem;
        m_dataitem = new DataItem(IDConstants.D_LOCALALARM,
                           IDConstants.T_MONITOR, m_lAlarm);
        m_dataPool.putData(m_dataitem);
      } else if (!isAlarm && wasAlarm) {
      // indicate transition from alarm to no alarm
      [...]
      }
  }
}
```

Figure 3.7   ATaG code listing for the Monitor task in Figure 2.20.

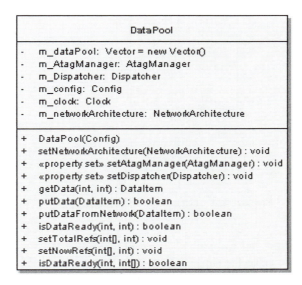

Figure 3.8 DataPool: UML class diagram.

3.3.3 DataPool

3.3.3.1 Service The `Datapool` provides two types of interfaces. The first interface includes the `get()` and `put()` commands used to add data items to and remove data items from the data pool, respectively. `putFromNetwork()` is a minor variant of the `put()` call that is invoked when the data item arrives from the network interface instead of being produced by an application task. The second interface supports a variety of calls used to query the state of data items in the pool; e.g., whether an instance of a data item is available or unavailable, active or inactive, etc. These terms are defined and explained in more detail in Section 3.3.3.3.

3.3.3.2 Interactions In the current design, the user tasks interact with the `DataPool` through the `get()` and `put()` calls. The `NetworkStack` invokes the `putFromNetwork()` call when a data item sent by another node arrives at the network interface. The `AtagManager` invokes the status query interface to determine if one or more tasks are ready to be scheduled for execution.

3.3.3.3 Implementation Data pool management involves handling concurrent accesses by more than one user level or system level task, maintaining reference counts for each instance of a data item in order to determine if a particular instance is active (i.e., still waiting to be consumed by one or more

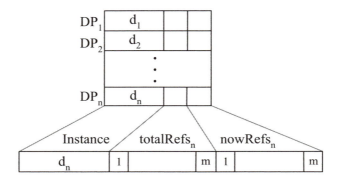

Figure 3.9   Structure of the data pool.

tasks that are scheduled for execution) or inactive (i.e., it can be overwritten when a new instance of the same type of data item is produced by a local task or received by the NetworkStack from another node). The get() function returns a copy of the requested data item to the caller and decrements the reference count of the associated item by one. put() adds an instance of a particular abstract data item to the data pool, unless the existing instance is active, in which case it returns without changing the data pool.

Let $\mathcal{AT} = \{t_1, \ldots, t_m\}$ be the set of abstract tasks, and let $\mathcal{AD} = \{d_1, \ldots, d_n\}$ be the set of abstract data items in the ATaG program. Atmost one instance of each data item can exist on a node at a given time. Let $\mathcal{DP} = \{DP_1, \ldots, DP_n\}$ be the set of entries of the datapool. Two boolean arrays — totalRefs$_i$ and nowRefs$_i$ — of length m each are associated with each entry DP_i (see Figure 3.9). When an instance of d_i is produced, these arrays help to keep track of (a) the dependent tasks for that data item and (b) the subset of those tasks that is scheduled for execution, respectively. The following explanation will clarify the role of these arrays.

When the node is initialized, the following is true:
totalRefs$_i$[j] $= false$, $1 \leq i \leq n, 1 \leq j \leq m$
nowRefs$_i$[j] $= false$, $1 \leq i \leq n, 1 \leq j \leq m$
d$_i$ $= NULL$, $1 \leq i \leq n$

An instance d_i can be in one or more of the following states at a given time:

- d_i is *available for task t_j* if totalRefs$_i$[j] $= true$.

- d_i is *available* if $\exists j$ s.t. d_i is available for task t_j.

- d_i is *unavailable for task t_j* if totalRefs$_i$[j] $= false$.

```
public synchronized DataItem getData(int taskID, int dataID) {
  DataItem t_dataItem = (DataItem) m_dataPool.get(dataID);
  if (t_dataItem.isAlive(taskID)) {
    t_dataItem.decrementRef(taskID);
    return t_dataItem;
  } else
    return null;
}
```

Figure 3.10   The getData() function.

- d_i is *unavailable* if d_i is unavailable for all tasks.

- d_i is *active* if (i) d_i is *available*, and (ii) $\exists j$ s.t. nowRefs$_i$[j] = *true*.

- d_i is *inactive* if (i) d_i is *available*, and (ii) $\forall j$, nowRefs$_i$[j] = *false*.

Suppose task t_j invokes get() for some d_i. get() succeeds if d_i is available for t_j, and it fails otherwise. If get() succeeds, nowRefs$_i$[j] and totalRefs$_i$[j] are both set to *false*, indicating that the task has consumed that instance.

Suppose task t_j invokes put() for some d_i. put() succeeds if d_i is unavailable or inactive, and it fails otherwise. If put() succeeds, the instance of d_i passed by the call occupies entry DP_i of the datapool. Next, the datapool manager determines if there are any dependent tasks for d_i, and further if any of those dependent tasks are *ready*. Let $\mathcal{DT}_i$ be the set of dependent tasks of d_i and let $\mathcal{RT}_i$ be the set of ready tasks at the time the put() was invoked, where $\mathcal{RT}_i \subseteq \mathcal{DT}_i \subset AT$. Before the successful put() returns, the datapool manager ensures that

$$\text{totalRefs}_i[j] \;=\; \text{true}, \forall t_i \in \mathcal{DT}_i,$$

and

$$\text{nowRefs}_i[j] \;=\; \text{true}, \forall t_i \in \mathcal{RT}_i.$$

An any-data task is scheduled for execution whenever any of its input data items become available. Similarly, an all-data task is scheduled for execution whenever all of its input data items become available. The destructive get() by task t_j of some d_i is ensured by setting the totalRefs$_i$[j] and nowRefs$_i$[j] to false. When a new instance of d_i is created, the corresponding put() will set these values to true again. Also, when a new instance d_i is produced, the number of tasks that are ready to consume that instance is reflected in the

```
public synchronized boolean putData(DataItem outputData) {
  int t_dataID = outputData.dataID();
  // If data item is active, do nothing and return "false"
  if (m_dataPool.elementAt(t_dataID) != null) {
    if (((DataItem) m_dataPool.get(t_dataID)).isActive())
      return false;
  }
  // Set time, date, node ID, and node coordinates of origin
  outputData.setDateStamp(m_clock.getDate());
  outputData.setTimeStamp(m_clock.getTime());
  outputData.setOriginID(m_config.myID());
  outputData.setOriginCoords(m_networkArchitecture.myCoords());
  // Add this to the datapool before calling AtagManager
  m_dataPool.add(t_dataID, outputData);
  // Call AtagManager who will set references and spawn tasks
  m_AtagManager.newInstanceProduced(outputData.producerID(),
                                    outputData.dataID());
  // Notify the dispatcher
  m_Dispatcher.newInstanceProduced(outputData);
  return true;
}
```

Figure 3.11   The putData() function.

number of true entries in $nowRefs_i$. Only when that instance is consumed by all the ready dependent tasks do the entries in $nowRefs_i$ become false and any put() allowed to overwrite that instance. Note that the use of two arrays is necessary because the fact that one or more tasks are dependent but not ready is reflected in the totalRefs array (e.g., an all-data task whose other data items are not yet available). The nowRefs array merely records whether a particular instance is being "actively" consumed by one or more dependent and ready tasks.

3.3.4   AtagManager

3.3.4.1 Service   The AtagManager supports a notification interface that is invoked whenever a new instance of a data item is produced by one of the tasks running on the node. A second interface provides answers to queries about the declarative part of the ATaG program—for example, the type and parameters of a particular channel annotation.

3.3.4.2 Interactions   The notification interface is used by the Datapool as part of processing a put() call from the user task or a putFromNetwork()

call from the `NetworkStack` component. The query interface for the declarative part of the ATaG program is used by the `Dispatcher` component.

3.3.4.3 *Implementation* `AtagManager` is charged with (i) internally representing the entire declarative part of the ATaG program (i.e., the task, data item, and channel declarations) and (ii) maintaining handles to the task code so that instances of abstract tasks mapped onto the node can be invoked when their firing conditions are met. Each abstract task declaration is stored as an instance of the `TaskDeclaration` class, and each abstract channel is stored as an instance of the `ChannelDeclaration` class. These two classes were discussed in Section 3.3.1.

The UML class diagram for `AtagManager` in Figure 3.13 shows the various attributes and methods in the current version of this class.

The constructor of `AtagManager` instantiates the `TaskDeclaration` and `ChannelDeclaration` classes—one for each abstract task and abstract channel in the ATaG program (Figure 3.14). This is one of the few methods in the runtime system that contain application-specific code which has to be generated during the software synthesis process.

When a new data item is added to the data pool using the `putData()` or `putDataFromNetwork()` function call, part of the processing of the function calls in the `DataPool` class involves an invocation of the `newInstance-Produced()` function of the `AtagManager`.

The code listing for this function in the current implementation of DART is shown in Figure 3.15. The arguments to this function are the ID of the abstract task that produced the data item and the ID of the data item that was produced.

The `AtagManager` first checks if the output channel corresponding to the task–data pair. If the output channel is marked as nonlocal, no further processing is performed because a data item produced by a nonlocal output channel is not meant to trigger any scheduling of dependent tasks on that node.

If the channel is not marked as nonlocal, the `AtagManager` determines the set of abstract tasks that are (a) mapped onto that node, and (b) dependent on the data item. The `totalRefs` array corresponding to the data item is now populated. The next task is to populate the `nowRefs` array and to schedule the suitable tasks for execution. The role of `totalRefs` and `nowRefs` arrays was discussed in Section 3.3.3.3.

For each dependent task that is assigned to (i.e., mapped onto) the node, the firing rule is determined. If the firing rule is `any-data`, the corresponding `nowRefs` entry is set to 1, and the task is immediately scheduled for execution. An `any-data` firing rule implies that the production of even one of the input data items is sufficient for the task to be scheduled, and there is no need to

```
public synchronized boolean putDataFromNetwork(DataItem outputData) {
  int t_dataID = outputData.dataID();
  // If data item is present and is active, do nothing and return "false"
  if (m_dataPool.elementAt(t_dataID) != null)
    if (((DataItem) m_dataPool.get(t_dataID)).isActive())
    return false;
  // If data originates from network, it is already stamped and should
  // not be changed
  // Add this to the datapool before calling AtagManager
  m_dataPool.add(t_dataID, outputData);
  // Call AtagManager who will set references and will spawn tasks
  m_AtagManager.newInstanceProduced(outputData.producerID(),
                                    outputData.dataID());
  return true;
}
```

Figure 3.12 The putDataFromNetwork function.

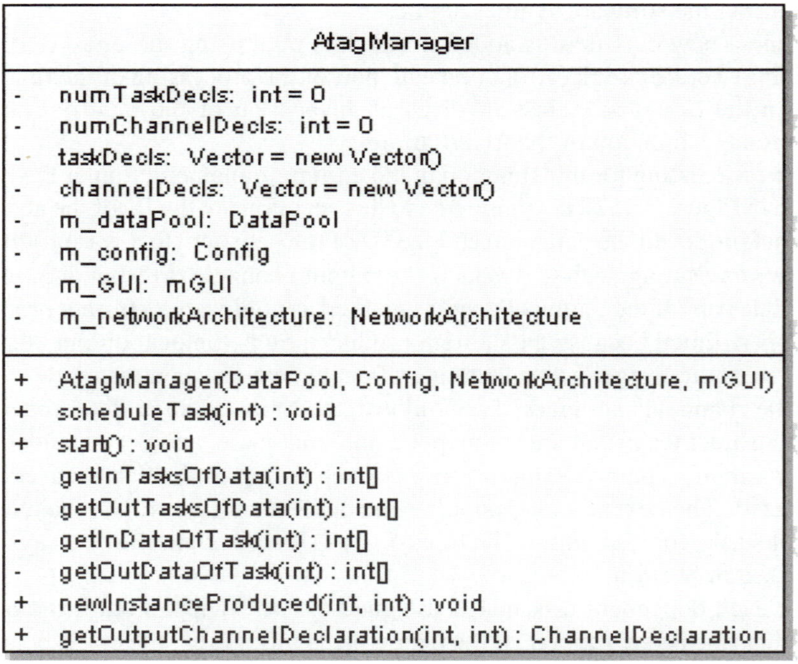

AtagManager

- numTaskDecls: int = 0
- numChannelDecls: int = 0
-- taskDecls: Vector = new Vector()
- channelDecls: Vector = new Vector()
- m_dataPool: DataPool
- m_config: Config
- m_GUI: mGUI
- m_networkArchitecture: NetworkArchitecture

+ AtagManager(DataPool, Config, NetworkArchitecture, mGUI)
+ scheduleTask(int) : void
+ start() : void
- getInTasksOfData(int) : int[]
- getOutTasksOfData(int) : int[]
- getInDataOfTask(int) : int[]
- getOutDataOfTask(int) : int[]
+ newInstanceProduced(int, int) : void
+ getOutputChannelDeclaration(int, int) : ChannelDeclaration

Figure 3.13 UML class diagram: AtagManager.

```
// ************ START OF AUTO-GENERATED CODE

numTaskDecls = 3;

taskDecls.add(IDConstants.T_SAMPLEANDTHRESHOLD,
   new TaskDeclaration(IDConstants.T_SAMPLEANDTHRESHOLD,
   new SampleAndThreshold(m_dataPool, m_config,
      m_networkArchitecture, m_GUI),
   Thread.MAX_PRIORITY-0, "NODES PER INSTANCE", false, 1,
   PERIODIC", 1, true));

taskDecls.add(IDConstants.T_LEADER,
   new TaskDeclaration(IDConstants.T_LEADER,
   new Leader(m_dataPool, m_config, m_networkArchitecture,
      m_GUI),
   Thread.MAX_PRIORITY-1, "NODES PER INSTANCE", false, 1,
   "ANYDATA", 3600, false));

taskDecls.add(IDConstants.T_SUPERVISOR,
   new TaskDeclaration(IDConstants.T_SUPERVISOR,
   new Supervisor(m_dataPool, m_config, m_networkArchitecture,
      m_GUI),
   Thread.MAX_PRIORITY-2, "ONE INSTANCE ON NODE ID", false, 0,
   "ANYDATA", 3600, false));

numChannelDecls = 4;

channelDecls.add(0, new ChannelDeclaration(
   IDConstants.T_SUPERVISOR, IDConstants.D_TARGETINFO, "INPUT",
   false, "push", "ALLNODES", 0));

channelDecls.add(1, new ChannelDeclaration(
   IDConstants.T_LEADER, IDConstants.D_TARGETALERT, "INPUT",
   false, "push", "", 0));

channelDecls.add(2, newChannelDeclaration(
   IDConstants.T_SAMPLEANDTHRESHOLD, IDConstants.D_TARGETALERT,
   "OUTPUT", true, "push", "NEIGHBORDISTANCE", 300));

channelDecls.add(3, new ChannelDeclaration(
   IDConstants.T_LEADER, IDConstants.D_TARGETINFO, "OUTPUT",
   true, "push", "", 0));

// ************** END OF AUTO-GENERATED CODE
```

Figure 3.14   Section of the AtagManager constructor that instantiates task and channel declaration classes. This code is automatically generated during software synthesis.

```
public void newInstanceProduced(int taskID, int dataID) {
    // If data is not local, do nothing locally when it is produced.
    ChannelDeclaration t_channelDecl = this.getOutputChannelDeclaration(taskID,
                                                                        dataID);
    if (t_channelDecl==null || !t_channelDecl.isLocal())
        return;

    // Data is marked 'local' and there is some output channel decl for it
    int[] dependentTasks = getOutTasksOfData(dataID);
    m_dataPool.setTotalRefs(dependentTasks, dataID);

    int[] nowRefs = new int[ArchConstants.MAXTASKS];

    for (int ctr = 0; ctr < dependentTasks.length; ctr++) {
        // If task is not dependent on this data item, go to next task
        if (dependentTasks[ctr] == 0)
            continue;
        // If task is dependent but is not assigned to this node,
        // go to next task
        if (!m_config.isTaskAssigned(ctr)) {
            continue;
        }
        TaskDeclaration thisTask = (TaskDeclaration) taskDecls.get(ctr);
        if ((thisTask.firingRule()).toUpperCase().equals("ANYDATA")) {
            // start any-data task
            nowRefs[ctr] = 1;
            thisTask.runTask();
        } else {
            // the task is all-data; check if other data is ready
            int[] flagArray = getInDataOfTask(ctr);
            boolean allOtherDataReady = true;
            for (int i = 0; i < flagArray.length; i++)
                if (flagArray[i] == 1 && (i != dataID) &&
                    !m_dataPool.isDataReady(taskID, i)) {
                    allOtherDataReady = false;
                    break;
                }
            if (allOtherDataReady) {
                // start all-data task
                nowRefs[ctr] = 1;
                thisTask.runTask();
            }
        }
    }
    // Only tasks that are actually enqueued should be flagged '1'
    m_dataPool.setNowRefs(nowRefs, dataID);
    return;
}
```

Figure 3.15   The `newInstanceProduced()` function of the AtagManager class.

check if other input data items (if any) for that task are ready or not. As mentioned earlier, an `any-data` task is responsible for handling situations where an input data item may not be available in the data pool. If the task has an `all-data` firing rule, the `AtagManager` checks if all other input data items for the task are ready, and it schedules the task for execution only if the condition is satisfied.

We do not worry about periodic tasks when the check for firing rule is performed. The first reason is that if a task has a `periodic` firing rule, it is triggered when the periodic timer expires and is not affected by the production of any input data items during the period between consecutive invocations. Also, the current version of DART does not support compound firing rules— for example, a task that is marked `periodic` ∨ `any-data`. Even after this support is included, such tasks will return `true` when the check for `any-data` firing is performed.

When the `newInstanceProduced()` function returns, all dependent tasks mapped onto that node whose firing conditions are met are in the scheduler's queue waiting for execution.

3.3.5   NetworkStack

3.3.5.1   Service   As indicated by its name, the basic service provided by the `NetworkStack` to the other components of the runtime is sending a data item to one or more nodes in the sensor network. The component is responsible for managing and initializing all the required protocols, which will typically include physical layer, medium access, and routing protocols. The `sendData()` functions shown in the class diagram (Figure 3.16) provide this service.

3.3.5.2   Interactions   The `Dispatcher` and the `NetworkArchitecture` components interact with the network stack. The former uses the interface to send data items to a set of nodes as indicated by the annotations of the output channel associated with that data item. The topology creation and management—as well as other, similar protocols in the latter—also access the transceiver through the `NetworkStack`.

3.3.5.3   Implementation   The implementation of this component is al- most entirely dependent on the target sensor node platform and the family of protocols available for that platform. The prototype version of DART is implemented primarily as a component of the simulation and visualization environment that accompanies the ATaG visual programming interface. Since the simulation is on a single machine, the interaction between independent DART processes representing different nodes of the network is through sock- ets on the simulation machine. The current DART implementation therefore opens a listener thread on a predefined socket number to simulate the receiver and a transmitter thread that sends the data items to the receiver sockets of the destination nodes.

In a "real" DART implementation (i.e., one that is deployed on a real or simulated sensor node that can directly communicate only with its 1-hop neigh- bors), protocols managed by the `NetworkArchitecture` will register their

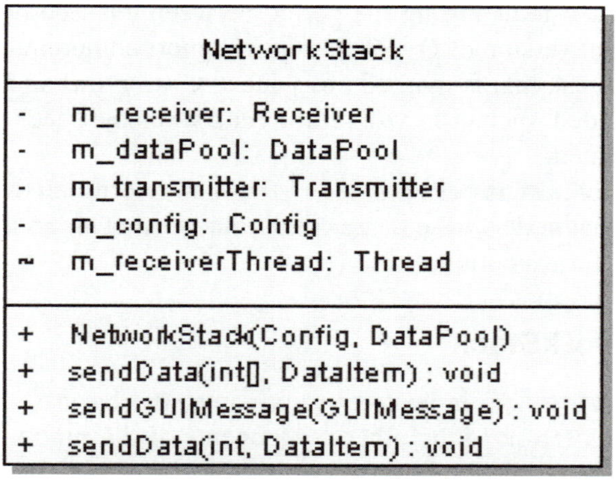

```
┌─────────────────────────────────────────────┐
│                NetworkStack                   │
├─────────────────────────────────────────────┤
│  -   m_receiver: Receiver                     │
│  -   m_dataPool: DataPool                     │
│  -   m_transmitter: Transmitter               │
│  -   m_config: Config                         │
│  ~   m_receiverThread: Thread                 │
├─────────────────────────────────────────────┤
│  +   NetworkStack(Config, DataPool)           │
│  +   sendData(int[], DataItem) : void         │
│  +   sendGUIMessage(GUIMessage) : void        │
│  +   sendData(int, DataItem) : void           │
└─────────────────────────────────────────────┘
```

Figure 3.16   UML class diagram: NetworkStack.

interest in specific message types that will correspond to the protocol-specific information exchanged between nodes. A message queue or similar mechanism will be used to exchange data between these protocols and the receiver and transmitter threads of the NetworkStack. This is similar to the active messages [54] model.

3.3.6   NetworkArchitecture

3.3.6.1   Service   NetworkArchitecture is responsible for managing all protocols and maintaining all information related to the *situatedness* of the node in the network. Situatedness implies a knowledge of the neighborhood composition, the role of the node in one or more virtual topologies (such as trees or meshes) that might be permanently or temporarily overlaid on all or part of the network. This service is provided through a query interface that translates architecture-independent specifications such as "ID of parent node," "IDs of child nodes," "geographic locations of nodes within 10 m of this node," etc., into the desired ID or location list. To summarize, this component provides context-awareness to the application-level and system-level components of the software system running on the sensor node.

3.3.6.2   Interactions   UserTask instances may optionally interact with the NetworkArchitecture to obtain information about the node's own coordinates, the composition of its neighborhood, its role (if any) in a virtual topology, etc. The Dispatcher also uses this query interface to translate annotations of output channels into list of node IDs and/or locations for transmitting the newly produced data item to its specified destinations. Finally, the NetworkArchitecture uses the services provided by the NetworkStack as required by the protocols it manages.

3.3.6.3 Implementation   As mentioned above, NetworkArchitecture is required as a separate (and important) component of DART because application-level tasks require information about the situatedness of the node in the target deployment. The architecture-independence and data-driven semantics of ATaG means that all the input and output by instances of abstract tasks are through the basic get() and put() primitives. All communication over the network is implicit in the channel annotations and is not directly controlled by the imperative portion of the ATaG program. However, an integral characteristic of networked sensing is that the processing of data items could be influenced by factors such as the location of the node, the density of sensor nodes in its region of deployment, etc. This means that if an abstract task with an input channel labeled *neighborhood-hops:1* is mapped onto a node, it is highly probable that the task code will want to know the composition of its 1-hop neighborhood in order to meaningfully interpret and suitably process the incoming data items represented by that channel.

The current implementation of NetworkArchitecture maintains information about a neighborhood whose "scope" is determined by the channel annotations of abstract tasks mapped onto that node. For example, let task A and task B be the only two abstract tasks of the ATaG program that are mapped onto a particular node. Suppose task A has an input channel with annotation *neighborhood-hops:3* and task B has an input channel with annotation *neighborhood-distance:50 m*. At compile time, the NetworkArchitecture component on that node is configured to collect information only about the union of the set of nodes within 3 hops of that node and the set of nodes within 50 m of that node. This ensures that the computation, communication, and storage resources required to maintain this information are justified by the (possible) utility of the information to tasks on that node. The set of function calls that form the query interface supported by this component are shown in the class diagram of Figure 3.17. Decisions about the activation of protocols for virtual topology formation are also taken at compile time. For instance, if the application requires a virtual tree topology, the programmer will presumably have identified the nodes that form the root and nonroot members of the tree in the network model that is provided to the compiler. The NetworkArchitecture modules on all or some of the nodes in the net-

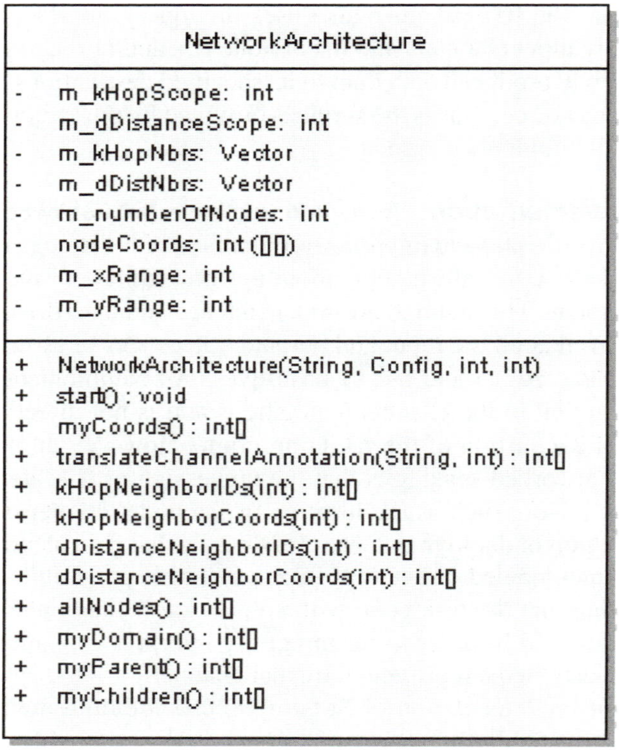

```
┌─────────────────────────────────────────────────┐
│               NetworkArchitecture               │
├─────────────────────────────────────────────────┤
│  -   m_kHopScope: int                            │
│  -   m_dDistanceScope: int                       │
│  -   m_kHopNbrs: Vector                          │
│  -   m_dDistNbrs: Vector                         │
│  -   m_numberOfNodes: int                        │
│  -   nodeCoords: int ([][])                      │
│  -   m_xRange: int                               │
│  -   m_yRange: int                               │
├─────────────────────────────────────────────────┤
│  +   NetworkArchitecture(String, Config, int, int) │
│  +   start() : void                              │
│  +   myCoords() : int[]                          │
│  +   translateChannelAnnotation(String, int) : int[] │
│  +   kHopNeighborIDs(int) : int[]                │
│  +   kHopNeighborCoords(int) : int[]             │
│  +   dDistanceNeighborIDs(int) : int[]           │
│  +   dDistanceNeighborCoords(int) : int[]        │
│  +   allNodes() : int[]                          │
│  +   myDomain() : int[]                          │
│  +   myParent() : int[]                          │
│  +   myChildren() : int[]                        │
└─────────────────────────────────────────────────┘
```

Figure 3.17   UML class diagram: NetworkArchitecture.

work will then be configured to start the tree formation protocols at node initialization time.

The four types of events involving the NetworkArchitecture that can occur at runtime are: A data item of interest to one of the protocols managed by this component arrives at the transceiver and is communicated to the protocol by the NetworkStack, a data item is sent to the NetworkStack by one of the protocols managed by this component; the query interface is invoked by an application level task; and the query interface is invoked by the Dispatcher.

3.3.7   Dispatcher

3.3.7.1   Service   The Dispatcher is responsible for transmitting any new instance of a data item produced on the node to other nodes (if any) indicated by the output channel annotation associated with the data item.

The component therefore supports a notification interface that consists of a `newInstanceProduced()` function.

3.3.7.2 *Interactions*

The `Datapool` is responsible only for managing the data pool. The `AtagManager` stores information about the declarative part of the program and also schedules the imperative portions for execution when appropriate. The `NetworkStack` manages the transceiver, and the `NetworkArchitecture` is in charge of situatedness information of the node.

None of the above components are assigned the task of determining where a particular data item produced on the node is to be sent. Hence, a new component—the `Dispatcher`—was created for coordinating between these modules and, when an instance of a data item is produced, sending it to the set of destination nodes as indicated in the ATaG program. Specifically, this component uses the query interface of `AtagManager` to obtain the output channel annotation associated with the data item, the translation service of the `NetworkArchitecture` to convert the channel annotation into a list of node IDs (or locations) that correspond to the annotation at that time, and the `send()` interface of the `NetworkStack` to actually dispatch the data to the destinations.

3.3.7.3 *Implementation*

The `Dispatcher` maintains handles to the `AtagManager`, `NetworkArchitecture`, and the `NetworkStack`, to be invoked in that order. When a new data item is produced, part of the `putData()` method of the `DataPool` class calls the `newInstanceProduced()` function of the `Dispatcher` module.

The code listing for this function is shown in Figure 3.20. First, we perform a sanity check to ensure that there is indeed an output channel declaration that corresponds to the production of this data item. The assumption is that there is exactly one such output channel. If more than one channel were allowed, additional record-keeping would be required to now determine which task produced the data item in question. This would increase the complexity of the runtime system. The ATaG syntax currently prohibits more than one output channel from being associated with a given data item for this reason.

The `Dispatcher` does not check if the output channel is local or nonlocal. That determination is the sole concern of the `AtagManager` because it affects the scheduling of dependent tasks (if any) on the local node. The `Dispatcher` merely checks if some channel annotation (interest) is associated with the output channel that can translate into one or more node IDs in the system. This information is obtained through the `AtagManager` module that stores the channel declaration and its associated annotations. If such an annotation

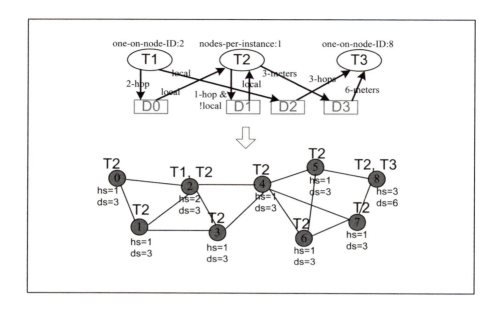

Figure 3.18   Hopscope.

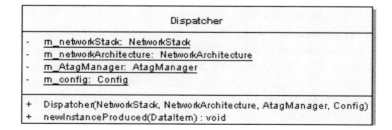

Figure 3.19   UML class diagram: Dispatcher.

```
public void newInstanceProduced(DataItem t_dataItem) {
  int[] nodeIDs = null;;
  int dataID = t_dataItem.dataID();
  ChannelDeclaration t_channelDecl =
                m_AtagManager.getOutputChannelDeclaration(
                        t_dataItem.producerID(), dataID);
  if (t_channelDecl == null) {
    // no output channel found for this data ID
    System.exit( -1);
  }
  String interest = t_channelDecl.interest();
  if (!(interest.toUpperCase().equals("NONE"))) {
    int interestParam = t_channelDecl.interestParam();
    // delegate the task of decoding the channel's annotation to
    // the NetworkArchitecture module
    nodeIDs = m_networkArchitecture.translateChannelAnnotation(interest,
                      interestParam);
    // NetworkArchitecture returns the list of nodeIDs (if any) that
    // correspond to the channel annotation
    if (nodeIDs != null) {
      // delegate the task of actually transmitting the data item to the
      // set of node IDs to the NetworkStack module
      m_networkStack.sendData(nodeIDs, t_dataItem);
    }
  }

  // Now check if any node IDs are specified as part of the config
  // file generated during compile time.
  nodeIDs = m_config.getDestinationOfData(dataID);
  if (nodeIDs != null)
    m_networkStack.sendData(nodeIDs, t_dataItem);
  return;
}
```

Figure 3.20   The newInstanceProduced() function of the Dispatcher module.

is found, it is passed to the NetworkArchitecture module that translates it into a (possibly empty) set of node IDs and returns the list to the Dispatcher.

3.4 CONTROL FLOW

The flow of control among the components of DART can be divided into two parts. The first is the set of activities that occur at *node initialization*. The second is the set of actions triggered during the course of *application execution* on that node. This set includes events that are generated by the user-level code (e.g., production and consumption of data items) and also events generated by components of the runtime system such as the protocols managed by the NetworkArchitecture component.

3.4.1 Startup

Figure 3.21 is the code listing for the startup routine that is executed when a node is initialized. This is the main routine in the `Startup` Java class that acts as the point of entry into the runtime system.

```
package atag.runtime;

import java.io.*;
import java.util.*;
import atag.runtime.config.*;
import atag.runtime.*;

public class Startup {

  public static DataPool m_dataPool;
  public static NetworkStack m_networkStack;
  public static NetworkArchitecture m_networkArchitecture;
  public static AtagManager m_AtagManager;
  public static Dispatcher m_Dispatcher;
  public static mGUI m_GUI;

  public static String networkFileName = "";

  public static int hopscope = 0;
  public static int distancescope = 0;

  public static void main(String argv[]) {
    Config m_config;
    m_config = parseCmdLineArgs(argv);
    m_dataPool = new DataPool(m_config);
    m_networkStack = new NetworkStack(m_config, m_dataPool);
    m_networkArchitecture = new NetworkArchitecture(networkFileName,
                              m_config, hopscope, distancescope);
    m_networkArchitecture.start();
    m_GUI = new mGUI(m_networkStack);

    m_AtagManager = new AtagManager(m_dataPool, m_config,
                              m_networkArchitecture, m_GUI);
    m_Dispatcher = new Dispatcher(m_networkStack, m_networkArchitecture,
                              m_AtagManager, m_config);
    m_dataPool.setAtagManager(m_AtagManager);
    m_dataPool.setDispatcher(m_Dispatcher);
    m_dataPool.setNetworkArchitecture(m_networkArchitecture);
    m_AtagManager.start();
    System.err.println(m_config.myID()+":␣started");
    return;
  }

}
```

Figure 3.21 The main routine of the `Startup` class.

Each module of DART is expected to implement a `start()` function that performs the basic initialization (if any) required for that module. Alternately, initialization may be performed in the constructor of that class in an object-oriented implementation. The initialization might involve memory allocation, initialization of variables, spawning of new threads for different protocols and services, etc.

A special `Startup` module of DART is the first to run when the node is turned on, and invokes the `start()` functions of the other modules. The code listing for the main function in the `Startup` module is shown in Figure 3.21.

First, the `Datapool` is started, which mainly involves allocating memory for each entry of the data pool corresponding to the different data items in the ATAG, and then marking the entries of the datapool as empty by suitably initializing the reference counts. Naturally, on resource-constrained platforms where dynamic memory allocation is not supported and the data structures of the data pool are determined and generated as part of software synthesis at compile time, the duties of the startup function will be reduced.

Next, the `NetworkStack` is started, which spawns the listener thread to accept incoming connections, and a transmitter thread to handle outgoing messages. The initialization, if any, needed by the MAC and routing protocols, and also the localization and time synchronization protocols, is performed before control returns to the `Startup` class. The code listing for the constructor of the `NetworkStack` is shown in Figure 3.22.

Now that the basic communication service with other nodes is available, the `NetworkArchitecture` module is started, which will spawn the protocol threads required for neighbor discovery, virtual topology construction, middleware services, etc. The startup of this module could be deemed complete when some minimum node state has accumulated; for example, all the information about the neighborhood is available. The current version of DART is designed primarily to support single-machine simulation and also does not include the protocols for local topology discovery. The entire network topology is read from a configuration file that is passed to the `Startup` module during initialization. We discuss this in more detail in Section 4.4.5.

Finally, the `ATaGManager` is started. This module traverses the list of user-level tasks assigned to that node, and it spawns all the tasks that are marked "run at initialization" by the programmer (see Figure 3.23). These will typically be the tasks that (periodically) produce the set of sensor readings that will then drive the rest of in-network processing. It is important to note that a periodic firing rule does not necessarily mean that the periodic execution of the task is started when the node is powered on. This is because the application

```
package atag.runtime;

import java.util.//;
import java.net.//;
import atag.runtime.config.//;
import atag.runtime.//;
import visualizer.//;

public class NetworkStack {
  private Receiver m_receiver;
  private DataPool m_dataPool;
  private Transmitter m_transmitter;
  private Config m_config;
  Thread m_receiverThread;

  public NetworkStack(Config t_config, DataPool dataPool) {
    // Startup routine in the constructor:
    // Startup the Receiver thread which will continually listen
    // on a specific socket number for data transfers from
    // other runtimes, and instantiate the Transmitter class
    // which will be used to send the data item to other nodes.
    //
    // Handle to the data pool is passed to the constructor
    // of the network stack because the Receiver thread
    // requires this handle to be able to call the
    // putDataFromNetwork method when a data item is
    //   received from other Transmitters.
    //
    m_dataPool = dataPool;
    m_config = t_config;
    m_receiver = new Receiver(t_config, dataPool);
    // start up the receiver when NetworkStack starts
    m_receiverThread = new Thread(m_receiver);
    m_receiverThread.start();
    m_transmitter = new Transmitter(t_config);
    return;
  }

  ...

}
```

Figure 3.22 The constructor and startup routine for the `NetworkStack`.

```
public class AtagManager {

  private int numTaskDecls = 0;
  private int numChannelDecls = 0;
  private Vector taskDecls = new Vector();
  private Vector channelDecls = new Vector();
  private DataPool m_dataPool;
  private Config m_config;
  private mGUI m_GUI;
  private NetworkArchitecture m_networkArchitecture;

  . . .

  public void start() {
    TaskDeclaration t_taskDecl;
    for (int ctr = 0; ctr < m_config.ntasks(); ctr++)
      if ((t_taskDecl =
                (TaskDeclaration) taskDecls.get(ctr)).runAtInit()) {
        // run task with ID ctr
        t_taskDecl.runTask();
      }
    return;
  }
  . . .
}
```

Figure 3.23   The startup routine for the `AtagManager`.

developer might want some task(s) to execute periodically only when a certain stage of the computation is reached or a certain event is detected. Hence, the boolean property "run at initialization" is to be specified for each abstract task (`false` by default) and only the tasks that have this property set to `true` will be started at node initialization, regardless of the firing rule. The application developer can use this mechanism to define application-level functionality that is executed only at initialization.

3.4.2   `get()` **and** `put()`

During the normal course of application execution, three main events can occur: (i) a `get()` invocation by a user task, (ii) a `put()` invocation by a user task, or (iii) a `put()` invocation by the receiver thread when a data item arrives from another node.

As explained in Section 3.3.3.3, a `get()` invocation merely results in the clearing of the corresponding entries of the `totalRefs` and `nowRefs` arrays of the data pool and, as a side effect, can change the state of a particular instance of a data item from available to unavailable, etc. In the current implementation, the processing of a get() call is performed entirely within the Datapool component, and none of the services offered by other DART components are used by Datapool.

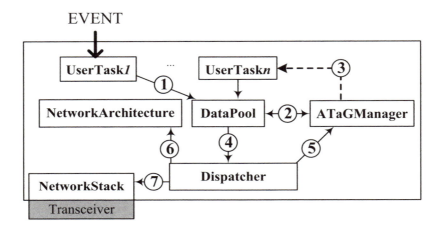

Figure 3.24   Flow of control on a put() invocation.

The processing of a put() call is more involved. Figure 3.24 shows the flow of control among DART components triggered by a put(). Steps 1 through 7 of the figure correspond to the following:

1. An instance of UserTask invokes put() for a particular abstract data item. The Datapool first checks if the corresponding data item can be safely added to the data pool—that is, if the data item is unavailable or inactive. If the addition fails, the put() returns with an error code and the contents of the data pool are not modified.

2. If the addition succeeds, Datapool invokes the newInstance-Produced() function of the AtagManager. The AtagManager checks if the output channel annotation for the newly produced data item contains *nonlocal*. If not, the AtagManager determines the list of tasks that depend on this data item and checks their firing rules. The arrow that denotes Step 2 is double-headed because this process involves some calls back to the Datapool to check the status of certain data items.

3. If one or more tasks are ready to be scheduled for execution, the Atag-Manager invokes the run() function provided by the Runnable interface supported by each UserTask.

4. The DataPool notifies the Dispatcher and returns control to the user task. Further processing by the Dispatcher can proceed in a separate thread of control.

5. The Dispatcher obtains the output channel annotation for the data item. If the ouptut channel is marked *local* only, the data item is not to be transmitted to any other nodes in the network and processing of the put() call terminates at this point.

6. If the output channel annotation indicates transmission of the data item to one or more nodes of the network, the Dispatcher queries the NetworkArchitecture to translate the channel annotation into a list of node IDs (or locations). Note that this assumes a scenario where the annotation is not translated into node IDs (or locations) at compile time, which typically will be the case if the network is dynamic. For a static network where some annotations are translated into node IDs (or locations) through an analysis of the network graph at compile time, the runtime translation will not be required. Instead, a list of node IDs (or locations) will be provided to the AtagManager instead of an untranslated channel annotation. In this case, Step 6 will be omitted.

7. Finally, the Dispatcher hands over the data item and the list of destinations to the NetworkStack for transmission.

The operating system and compiler support for the platform on which DART is implemented heavily affects the (a) design and implementation of the components and (b) the management of details of the control flow. For instance, a real-time operating system such as μC/OS-II includes a preemptive priority-based scheduler and support for multi-threading, which is not available in an operating system such as TinyOS for resource constrained sensor nodes. Also, if μC/OS-II is the choice of operating system, the DART implementation (and the software synthesis process) will be affected by the target processor.

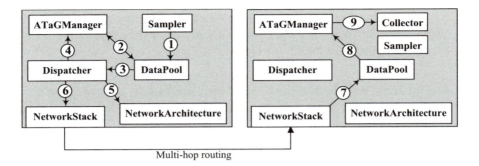

Figure 3.25 Centralized data collection: control flow at the sampler and collector nodes.

The description of the DART architecture and details of its control flow are hence intended to be a guide (template) for implementing system-level support for the ATaG programming model, with DART implementations on different sensor node platforms differing from another in the details.

The third type of event – an invocation of the putFromNetwork() call by the receiver thread of the NetworkStack—is handled in much the same way as a local invocation, except that the Dispatcher is not part of the loop.

3.4.3 Illustrative example

In centralized data collection, a Sampler task is hosted on each node of the network, and a Collector task is hosted on a single designated root node. The Sampler runs periodically and produces a data item that is to be routed to the Collector at the root node. The ATaG program for this behavior therefore consists of two abstract tasks and one data item.

Figure 3.25 depicts the intranode and internode flow of control whenever a data sample is created at a nonroot node (left) and communicated to the root node (right). The individual steps have already been explained in the previous subsection. In this example, the invocation of a put() by the Sampler only results in execution of six of the seven steps discussed in the earlier section. This is because the AtagManager does not invoke any task on that node, since no task dependent on the Sampler is mapped on the nonroot node. When the data item arrives at the network interface of the root node, the NetworkStack adds it to the data pool, which leads to the scheduling of the Collector task that consumes the newly arrived data item sent by the Sampler.

3.5   FUTURE WORK

A fully functional albeit simplified version of DART (DART-J) intended for single-machine simulation has been implemented in Java. DART-J has a modified network interface that communicates through sockets on the local host. Each instance of DART is also aware of the entire network architecture at startup (by reading from a file); and the protocols for neighborhood discovery, etc., are not required and not implemented. An ANSI C version of DART (DART-C) has also been partly implemented for a sensor node with a PIC18LF8720 microcontroller, 3840 bytes of RAM, 128KB of program memory, and 1KB of EEPROM. DART-C is designed for the MicroC/OS-II real-time operating system. Hardware design of the node, implementation of low-level APIs, and software development of the runtime is proceeding in concert and is not yet complete. We do not expect to implement an ATaG runtime on the TinyOS operating system in the near future, primarily because of the lack of the prerequisite mechanisms required by DART to guarantee ATaG semantics. We believe that using a small-footprint, widely available component-based operating system that provides the necessary mechanisms is an option as good or better than first implementing these mechanisms as a set of extra nesC modules for TinyOS and then layering the application-level task code on top of these modules.

We now discuss some areas of future work for DART. These are in addition to the modifications to the DART design and implementation that will be required to support the proposed enhancements to ATaG (Section 2.6).

3.5.1   Lazy compilation of channel annotations

The destination(s) of a particular data item produced on a node is indicated in the ATaG program in an architecture-independent manner. The actual translation of an annotation such as *neighborhood-distance:10 m* into the list of nodes that fall within the 10 m radius of a particular node in the network can take place at compile time or at run time. If the network deployment is static and known at design time, the `AtagManager` can be directly supplied with a list of source or destination IDs corresponding to input and output channels, respectively. The `NetworkArchitecture` does not need to maintain and update this information, thereby saving the resources required to run the necessary protocols. If the network is dynamic, this translation must happen at run time.

The application developer does not care if the translation is eager (compile-time) or lazy (runtime), as long as the communication between tasks in the network occurs according to the scheme indicated in the ATaG program. Indeed, this is the essence of architecture independent high-level programming. It also means that the decisions about lazy or eager evaluation of annotations, frequency of refreshing node state in a lazy evaluation scenario, etc., is entirely upto the compilation framework and the runtime system.

One of the areas of future work in this context is to define a technique to minimize the cost of execution (using a suitably defined metric) by selecting the evaluation policy for each annotation. The evaluation policy will determine whether the compilation of an annotation is eager, lazy, or a combination of both. For lazy compilation, it will also determine how frequently the `NetworkArchitecture` will update the relevant information about the neighborhood.

3.5.2   Automatic priority assignment for task scheduling

When the macroprogram is translated into a set of node-level program, it is critical for the compiler to guarantee that the semantics of the macroprogram are honored by the distributed system. Some of the ATaG semantics governing the production and consumption of data items are the responsibility of the data pool manager in the runtime system. Semantics of interest at the compiler level relate to task scheduling. Specifically, the compiler must guarantee atomic execution of application-level tasks and breadth-first execution of the task graph mapped onto a node. These semantics are motivated by the nature of "typical" data-driven sensor network applications and have been discussed in detail in Section 2.4.

Target platforms for DART are required to provide a preemptive, priority-based scheduler. Any platform that can host a Java virtual machine or a real-time operating systems such as μC-OS II is a suitable target. With such a scheduler, tasks are assigned priorities and the task with the highest priority at any given time executes. If another task with a still higher priority becomes ready for execution, the running task is preempted and the new task is given control of the CPU. The execution semantics of the abstract task graph can be ensured by suitably assigning priorities to tasks, depending on the scheduling policy to manage the execution.

For a given ATaG program, the compiler should perform this priority assignment after the task placement phase. Not all abstract tasks in the program are instantiated on every node. Each node is assigned a subset of the tasks, depending on the placement annotations and any application-level optimizations performed during compilation. For a given node, each task in the assigned set has a firing rule and some data dependencies. Also, some of the data items might actually be produced on other nodes and injected into the local data pool through the network interface. The arrival times of such external data items cannot be predicted, and the task can become ready for execution at any time. Maintaining the execution semantics in the face of uncertain arrival times of external data items, in addition to the dependencies of tasks on that node, is a challenge that needs to be tackled.

Also, the size of an ATaG program in terms of the number of abstract tasks depends on the application. Not all schedulers support a large number of distinct priority levels. For instance, a Java thread's priority is specified with an integer from 1 (lowest) to 10 (highest); also the real-time specification for java (RTSJ) [49] offers 28 strictly enforced priority levels, whereas μC-OS II [39] allows more than 50. Hence, another subproblem is that of performing priority assignment by intelligent allocation from a limited number of priority levels. We will implement a mechanism for limited-range priority assignment to abstract tasks, based on the observation that not all tasks will become active at a given time, and it might be acceptable to assign the same priority to more than one task as long as they do not become ready for execution at the same time.

CHAPTER 4

PROGRAMMING AND SOFTWARE SYNTHESIS

This chapter describes the process of application development with ATaG. The declarative part of the ATaG program is specified through an easy-to-use graphical interface. Although a variety of representations are possible for specifying the declarative part of an ATaG program, we chose the graphical interface because of the benefit of providing a concrete syntax that is identical to the abstract syntax, thereby eliminating the learning curve for the application developer.

The imperative part, consisting of the code associated with each abstract task and abstract data item, is provided by the user, with assistance from a code template generator tool. Software synthesis, simulation, and visualization is performed by tools that are launched from the visual programming interface. The GUI is based on the Generic Modeling Environment toolsuite [21]. We first introduce the GME toolsuite and then describe how GME was used to implement a programming and software synthesis mechanism for ATaG.

Architecture-Independent Programming for Wireless Sensor Networks
By Amol B. Bakshi, Viktor K. Prasanna

4.1   TERMINOLOGY

Model integrated computing (MIC): MIC is an approach for development of complex systems that is based on capturing all the relevant system information in a structured form (models) and using the model information to drive a set of domain-specific tools for analysis and synthesis.

Model: Models are abstractions that allow the representation and manipulation of various aspects of the underlying system. The set of parameters captured in the model depends entirely on the intended usage of the model information and the domain of application. The term "model" is commonly used to refer to mathematical models that describe a system through (a) a set of variables that represent properties of interest and (b) a set of equations that describe the relationships between the variables. We use the term "model" to denote structural models and not mathematical models. A domain-specific structural modeling language defines the basic building blocks that are available to the designer to describe a particular system in that domain. The domain-specific language also implicitly includes the semantics of each building block and the semantics of relationships between the building blocks. Examples of relationships include association, containment, and physical connectivity.

The Generic Modeling Environment (GME): GME is a configurable graphical toolsuite that supports MIC. The configuration of the environment to support domain-specific modeling is done in a formal manner through the use of metamodels. The metamodeling language is the UML class diagram notation. GME allows rapid creation of domain-specific modeling environments that are used by designers to describe systems in that domain, performs desired transformations on the model data, and drives external tools with the model information as input. *Model interpreters* are the software components that interface with the model database and manipulate and otherwise use the model information.

4.2   META-MODELING FOR THE ATaG DOMAIN

4.2.1   Objectives

GME was used to create a programming and software synthesis for the ATaG model. The objective of the customized graphical programming environment was to provide the following basic capabilities:

- The ability to visually specify the declarative portion of the ATaG program. This means that the abstract task, abstract data, and abstract channel are the basic building blocks of the structural model of the ATaG program, and the annotations associated with each should also be specified (or selected from a list of predefined values).

- The ability to create a library of ATaG programs (also called "behaviors") and compose larger applications by selecting and concatenating programs from this library.

- The ability to visually specify the parameters of the target network deployment, such as the number of nodes and the coordinates of each node, node identifiers, radio ranges, etc.

- The ability to create a library of network descriptions that will typically correspond to existing deployments, similar to the library of ATaG programs.

- The ability to indicate which set of ATaG programs is to be compiled on which of the network models, as well as to invoke the software synthesis tools for generating customized code to be downloaded and deployed on each node in the selected target.

A visual interface for drawing the ATaG program eliminates the need for the programmer to learn a new syntax and also makes it easy to comprehend the structure of an existing program. The ability to create libraries of behaviors and deployments allows reuse of existing applications as components of larger applications, and it also allows the same application to be compiled for a different network. At the highest level of abstract, as will be shown in the following sections, ATaG programming translates into the selection of one or more behaviors from the program library, the selection of one network description from the deployment library, and the invocation of software synthesis tools integrated into the development environment. The software synthesis methodology itself is structured in such a way that the imperative portions of existing ATaG programs (i.e., the code associated with the tasks and data items) can be reused. Ultimately, this means that *if a programmer wishes to merely combine existing behaviors to form a larger application, and compile it for one of the existing network descriptions, not a single line of code needs to be written.* This feature is one of the biggest strengths of the ATaG model and is the best demonstration of the advantages of using the data-driven programming paradigm for modularity and composability, with mixed imperative–declarative program specification for separation of concerns.

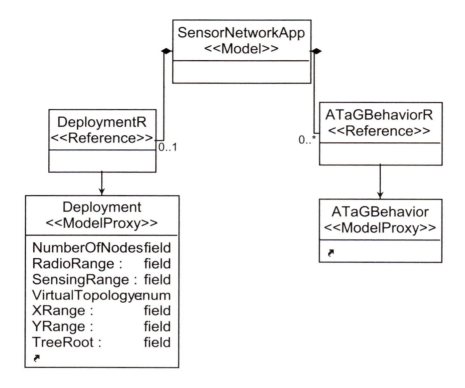

Figure 4.1 GME metamodel: Sensor network application consists of a set of behaviors mapped onto one target deployment.

The MetaGME paradigm that is used to specify the domain-specific meta-models provides basic building blocks that are used to define the structure of valid models in the target domain. Examples of the building blocks include atom, model connection, reference, etc. The GME users' manual explains the metamodeling and modeling concepts and processes in more detail. Here, we present the metamodels that are defined to create the ATaG programming environment.

4.2.2 Application model

The modeling paradigm for the ATaG programming environment is defined as follows. As shown in Figure 4.1, the sensor network application consists of one or more behaviors and one network description. All behaviors to be synthesized onto the target network are required to be part of this top-level model. The individual behaviors are represented as models named ATaGBehavior.

As mentioned in earlier sections, one of the advantages of the data-driven paradigm is the composability of programs by literally concatenating sub-programs. This property allows the creation of libraries of ATaG programs for different behaviors, which can be easily composed into the desired application by the end user. To support this drag-and-drop composition of applications from existing libraries, we do not include the ATaGBehavior models directly into this high-level model. Instead, the top-level model contains references to behaviors and a reference to a network description. References act as pointers to other entities; in this case, the actual behaviors and the network description are stored separately in the library and the programmer includes the behaviors in the application by simply pointing to it. In the figure, the ATaGBehaviorR entity is a reference to an ATaGBehavior model, and the DeploymentR entity is a reference to a Deployment model, each of which is now explained in more detail.

The declarative portion of the ATaG program is described by instantiating the **ATaG** model. The structure of the model is shown in Figure 4.2. The model consists of Tasks and DataItems, corresponding to abstract tasks and abstract data items, respectively. The annotations for tasks and data items are specified as attributes of the models. As shown in the figure, attributes of the Task model include firing rule, type of instantiation, priority of the task, whether the task should be executed at node initialization, etc. The fact that an attribute is associated with a model does not necessarily mean that the programmer has to specify its value. Attributes such as TaskID and Priority could be computed at compile time for a particular application and then recorded in the model for inspection by the programmer. Note that the current version of the metamodel is a prototype primarily meant to demonstrate the power of visual programming with ATaG. Some attributes in the current model are placeholders for information that is not used by the mapping and software synthesis tools. As the programming paradigm evolves, the metamodels will evolve accordingly.

One of the main attractions of using the GME toolkit for designing the ATaG programming environment is the ease of modifying the modeling paradigm and automatically generating an updated graphical modeling environment. Attributes of various types (boolean, integer, string, etc.) can be associated with the metamodel entities (atoms, models, connections, references, etc.) by specifying them in the 'Attributes' aspect of the metamodeling environment. Figure 4.3 shows the Attributes aspect of the ATaG metamodel. The FiringRule

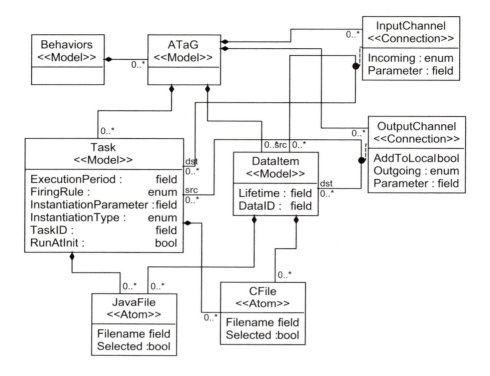

Figure 4.2 GME metamodel: Modeling paradigm for the ATaG program (declarative).

is an enum attribute, which means that a list of valid selections is prespecified in the metamodel. The lower right section of the GME window in Figure 4.3 shows the specification of allowable values for the firing rule, in accordance with the ATaG semantics in Section 2.4.

4.2.3 Network model

The application developer describes a target network as an instance of the **Deployment** model. The structure of the Deployment model is shown in Figure 4.4. The description of the target deployment can be separated into network-level parameters and node-level parameters. Examples of network-level parameters include: number of nodes, radio range (assuming all nodes have a fixed radio range), the real or virtual X and Y coordinate range of the localization system, etc.

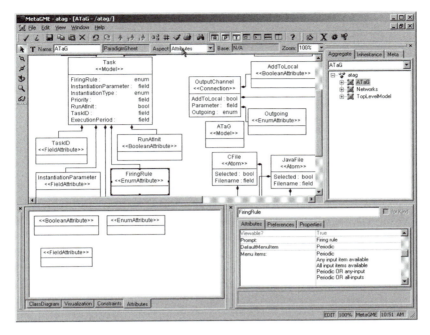

Figure 4.3   GME metamodel: Specifying annotations for tasks and data items.

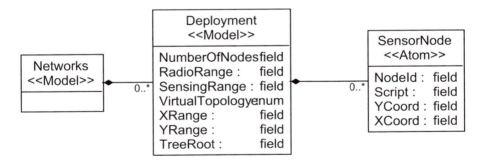

Figure 4.4   GME metamodel: Modeling paradigm for the network.

The set of parameters that are captured in our current metamodel are meant to be representative of the information that might be required for the compiler to synthesize an ATaG program on that deployment. By categorizing radio range as a network-level parameter, we assume that all nodes have identical radios with fixed radio range, and hence the radio range can be specified at the network level and not for the individual node. The X and Y coordinate range also implies that nodes are localized in a two-dimensional space. The advantage of using a configurable modeling environment such as GME is that the metamodel (and hence the programming environment) can be easily modified by including additional network-level or node-level parameters as desired.

4.3 THE PROGRAMMING INTERFACE

This section describes the use of the visual programming environment configured by the GME metamodels discussed above. The sequence of steps to be followed by the programmer can be summarized as follows.

Step I. Create a library of ATaG behaviors: An ATaG behavior is a standalone ATaG application, consisting of abstract taks, abstract data items, and input and output channels and their annotations. When part of a library, it can also be concatenated with other behaviors in the library and/or user-defined behaviors. We require the application developer who wishes to define his/her own ATaG behavior to first add it to the library and then import that behavior and any of the other preexisting behaviors from the library into the overall application.

Behaviors are created in the GME environment by navigating to the `Beha-viors` model and instantiating a model of type `ATaG` from the parts browser window at the lower right of the GME interface. The model instance is then renamed as desired. The programmer then double-clicks on the renamed `ATaG` model instance and is presented with a new set of building blocks that correspond to abstract tasks and data items. The programmer then specifies the declarative part of the behavior by simply dragging the desired number of tasks and data items from the parts browser to the model editing pane. Each task and data item can be renamed by selecting it and editing the values in the attributes window on the lower right of the main GME window.

Output channels are created by selecting the connection mode from the GME mode bar, clicking first on the producer task and then on the produced data item. When the channel (connection) is created, its directionality is indicated by an arrow pointing to the data item. Selecting the channel displays another set of editable attributes in the attribute browser, corresponding to channel annotations. Input channels are specified in a similar manner by first selecting the data item and then the consumer task.

Step II. Create a library of network descriptions: Similar to the library of ATaG programs (behaviors), the programming environment allows the creation of a library of deployment descriptions. Each network description could correspond to some real deployment that will host the application, or simply a fictitious network deployment designed solely for testing the ATaG program behavior through functional simulation.

A network description will consist of network-level parameters such as the number of nodes, the scope of the coordinate system (if any) in terms of X and Y coordinate range, the availability of protocols for establishing virtual topology, etc. This information will be used to translate the ATaG annotations for that particular network and will also be used to determine if a particular ATaG behavior selected by the programmer has a valid mapping onto the selected target deployment. For instance, if the ATaG program uses the annotations 'parent' and 'children' on the channels, the network description must indicate (a) the availability of protocols to establish a virtual tree topology and (b) any parameters required by that protocol, such as the identity of the root node of the tree. Similar to the library of behaviors, if the desired network description already exists, this step can be omitted.

The network description currently captures only the number of nodes, their X and Y coordinates, the span of the virtual coordinate system along the two dimensions, the radio range, and sensing range of the sensor interface on each node. The network is assumed to be homogeneous in that all nodes are considered to be identical. We also assume an "ideal" environment and do not model the effect of obstacles or hostile terrain on network connectivity. If the ATaG compiler is to be made sophisticated enough to choose or customize the lower-layer network protocols based on such information, the necessary attributes can be added to the programming interface. We also do not capture any node-level attributes relating to resource availability such as the energy available to each node.

Step III. Compose the application and select the target network: After the new behaviors (if any) are added to the existing library of programs and the desired target deployment is modeled, the programmer has to compose the application. Application composition is simply the graphical concatenation of behaviors from the library.

In the GME window, the programmer instantiates the desired number of references to ATaG behaviors and one reference to the network model. Then each behavior reference is associated with (bound to) the actual behavior from the library, and the reference to the target deployment is bound to one of the existing network models. More than one behavior references can be included but only one network reference must be present.

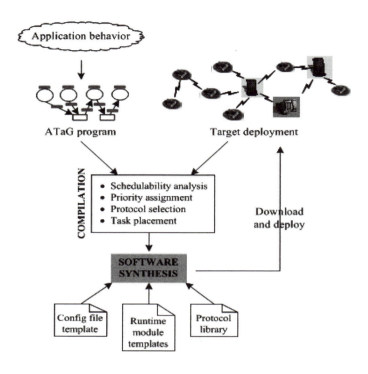

Figure 4.5 Application development with ATaG.

Step IV. Invoke the compilation and software synthesis tools: After application composition, the programmer launches the compilation and software synthesis tool, which guides him/her through a series of decisions, culminating in the generation of configuration files, customized DART components, scripts to launch the simulation and visualization tools, etc. This process will be described in more detail in Section 4.4.3.

One of the intermediate steps in this process is the automatic generation of code skeletons for the abstract tasks and abstract data items, which are to be filled in by the programmer. We expect that each behavior that is contributed to the library is also associated with its imperative portion (the classes for the task and data items). If the programmer is using existing behaviors from the library and not defining new ATaG programs, then the generation of code skeletons is not required. In other words, for the end user who wishes only to compile existing behaviors onto a new or existing networks, ATaG does not require even a single line of code to be written.

4.4 COMPILATION AND SOFTWARE SYNTHESIS

In this section, we describe the rudimentary compilation mechanism in the current ATaG programming environment, and the support for automatic software synthesis that generates skeleton code for user tasks and also individually customizes the runtimes on each sensor node such that the "macro"-level intent of the programmer, as expressed by the ATaG program, is preserved when the program is translated onto a distributed system.

Rudimentary compilation means that the compiler only ensures functionally correct translation of task and channel annotations in the ATaG program. No attempt is made to evaluate or optimize the performance of the synthesized application. Defining an optimizing compiler for sensor network applications is an exciting area for future work and outside the scope of this discourse.

In the context of distributed computing in general and sensor networking in particular, the phrase "correct translation" can have a multitude of implications and it is therefore necessary to clarify its precise meaning in the ATaG context. "Correct"-ness in the ATaG compilation process merely means that the semantics of task and channel annotations as defined in Section 2.4 are preserved when the program is translated for the distributed sensor network. For instance, the compiler ensures that the density of task instantiation and the firing rules as specified in the ATaG program are preserved for the particular target network and runtimes. Atomicity of task execution is guaranteed by suitably assigning priorities for task scheduling on the individual sensor node. The assignment of priorities is the responsibility of the end user, and the current compiler does not incorporate mechanisms to automatically assign priorities.

For channel annotations, the compiler ensures that the propagation of data items in the deployed network is in accordance with the declarative intent of the channel annotations. If data items are routed, in the ATaG program, to tasks that are mapped onto specific, hard-coded node IDs, then the compiler generates specific instructions for the runtimes on the producer nodes to transmit the data item to the specific node ID.

Correctness does not imply anything more than the above translation. ATaG, like almost all the programming languages, only provides building blocks with well-defined syntax and semantics to the programmer. The programmer is solely responsible for translating the high-level application functionality (such as "track an elephant") into the sequence of communication and computation that must take place in the network to accomplish the objective. By providing high-level abstractions to concisely specify this communication and computation mechanism in an architecture-independent manner, ATaG attempts to make the task of application development easier for the average sensor network programmer.

It is entirely possible to write incorrect programs in ATaG, like in almost every other programming language. The only guarantee of "correctness" that the compiler attempts to provide is that the distributed algorithm represented by the macroprogram will be accurately translated into the distributed computing substrate. It does not and cannot guarantee that the macroprogram accurately represents the high-level intent of the application developer concerning the semantics of the networked sensing application.

The software that runs on each node of an ATaG-programmed system consists of: (i) user-supplied code for each abstract task and abstract data item, (ii) components of the runtime system that are independent of the particular ATaG program being synthesized, and (iii) components of the runtime system that need to be customized for the particular ATaG program being synthesized. Examples of the "standard" DART components are the `Datapool`, the `Dispatcher`, the `NetworkArchitecture`, and the `NetworkStack`. The `AtagManager` has to be customized for the application because the information it maintains includes the task and channel annotations, and handles to the user level code.

If dynamic memory allocation is not supported on the target platform, the data structures of `Datapool` need to be customized for the abstract data items that will be generated and consumed on that node—the `Datapool` needs to be customized accordingly. However, in the current implementation of DART in Java, this customization is not required because the data pool stores data items as instances of a generic class `DataItem`.

Also, the current implementation of DART for single-machine simulation purposes does not require customization of the services for the `NetworkArchitecture` module because the protocols for neighborhood maintenance and topology formation are replaced with equivalent code that reads from a configuration file on the disk and obtains the topology information. In a "deployable" version of DART, some code in this component is likely to be customized for the requirements of the ATaG program.

If some sensor nodes in the target system have a wired network connection while others communicate through a variety of wireless network interfaces, the suitable `NetworkStack` will have to be selected for each node, based on the information provided in the network model. Currently, this component requires no customization because the network interfaces are assumed to be homogeneous, and no per-node optimization at compile time or runtime is performed in this component. We now describe the compilation and software synthesis process in more detail.

4.4.1   Translating task annotations

The output of the compilation process is (i) a set of config files for each node in the network, (ii) customized constructor for the `AtagManager`, and (iii) the network topology file in the specific format required by the `NetworkArchitecture` module to initialize itself.

Figure 4.6 is an excerpt of the GME model interpreter that interprets the task annotations in the context of the target network and generates config files for each node of the network. In this code listing, only the task annotations *one-on-node-ID:n* and *nodes-per-instance:1* are being parsed. This simple code listing is from an early version of the ATaG compiler designed to demonstrate architecture-independent programming for a specific case study. The DART runtime and the compiler are being continually extended to parse an increasing set of task placement annotations, and the latest code will be available through the ATaG website. Also, the language in which the model interpreter is written is (naturally) independent of the language of implementation of DART. Currently, the code generation for DART is also performed through a model interpreter written in the same language (Java). Other language options such as C++ are also available for the model interpreter. Future compilers and code generators for ATaG might not be written in Java.

4.4.2   Automatic software synthesis

Software synthesis is performed through model interpreters in the GME environment. Model interpreters are software components that can access the information entered graphically by the user by using an API provided by the GME toolsuite. The building blocks—such as Atom, Model, Reference, and Connection—provided by the GME metamodeling environment do not have associated domain-specific semantics. It can also be argued that the building blocks—such as ATaGBehaviorR, Deployment, SensorNode, Task, and Data—provided by the domain-specific modeling environment also do not have any inherent semantics except in the mind of the programmer. It is the model interpreters written for a particular modeling paradigm that encapsulate the semantics of the domain by suitably "interpreting" the model components and parameters to accomplish the desired domain-specific objective.

```
// Config file generation in the GME model interpreter
public void GenerateConfigFiles() {
    configStrings = new String[ntopo.nnodes];
    ...
    // Look at all task annotations and assign them to the
    // suitable nodes; parse only two types for now
    for (int i=0; i<atagInfo.numTasks(); i++) {
        TaskInfo t = atagInfo.taskInfo(i);
        String instType = t.instType();
        int instParam = t.instParam();
        if ((instType.toUpperCase().equals("NODES␣PER␣INSTANCE")) &&
                (instParam == 1))
            for (int j=0; j < ntopo.nnodes; j++) {
                t.assign(j);
                configStrings[j] += t.id() + "␣";
            }
        else if (instType.toUpperCase().equals("ONE␣INSTANCE␣ON␣NODE␣ID"))
        {
            t.assign(instParam);
            configStrings[instParam] += t.id() + "␣";
        }
    }
    // generate instructions for data routing
    for (int i=0; i<atagInfo.numData(); i++) {
        DataInfo d = atagInfo.dataInfo(i);
        ...
        // determine where the producer tasks for this data are mapped
        for (int j=0; j<outChannels.length; j++) {
            TaskInfo producer = atagInfo.taskInfo(outChannels[j].task());
            producerMap = producer.assignment();
        }
        // determine placement of consumer tasks
        if (inChannels.length == 0)
            continue;
        for (int j=0; j<inChannels.length; j++)
         if ((inChannels[j].interest().toUpperCase()).equals("ALL␣NODES"))
         {
            TaskInfo consumer = atagInfo.taskInfo(inChannels[j].task());
            int[] destinations = consumer.assignment();
            for (int k=0; k<destinations.length; k++)
                consumerMap.add(new Integer(destinations[k]));
        }
        // generate -senddata for config file
        ...
    }
}
```

Figure 4.6   Generating config files for each node of the network.

In our case, the objectives of model interpretation are:

1. To allow the application developer to visualize the network deployment
   in two dimensions and also inspect node connectivity and sensing coverage. This facility allows the application developer to quickly create

and inspect dummy sensor network deployments for application testing purposes. It also provides a more intuitive interface for visualizing the deployment than the GME interface, which is not very friendly for visualizing spatial distribution.

2. To generate code skeletons for each abstract task (if required) for the user to populate with application-specific code. Generating the code skeleton allows the application developer to focus on writing the application-specific functionality without worrying about details of the glue code that is necessary to integrate the user level tasks into the DART runtime system.

3. To customize DART components such as the `AtagManager`.

4. To generate files and scripts to configure and launch the simulation and visualization environment.

The compilation and software synthesis process is started by invoking a single model interpreter—the initial dialog box is shown in Figure 4.7. Similar dialog boxes guide the user through the process. If the application developer wants to visualize the deployment, a display similar to the one shown in Figure 4.8. The visualization is required because the GME model for a deployment is basically a container for atoms of type *SensorNode*. Inspecting the GME model does not give an idea of the distribution of the nodes in the (two-dimensional) field, the connectivity of the network as determined by the communication range of each transceiver, and the degree of coverage of each type of sensing interface in the network.

The model interpreter then generates code skeletons for each abstract task in the application, if desired by the programmer. If a new ATaG behavior is being developed and the associated code is therefore to be written, the developer can create a dummy application by (a) including only the ATaG behavior being created and (b) choosing to generate code skeletons for the abstract tasks and data items. The code synthesizer analyzes (i) the I/O dependencies between abstract tasks and data and (ii) the firing rules for the abstract task, and it generates a generic code skeleton as shown in Figure 4.9.

The programmer can then add application-specific code to the body of the Java class, define static variables to store state information across invocations, etc. The remainder of the software synthesis consists of customizing the constructor of the `AtagManager` (see Figure 3.14) and generating configuration files that provide the basic startup information to each DART process when it is launched as part of the simulation. The details of simulation are discussed in Section 4.4.3.

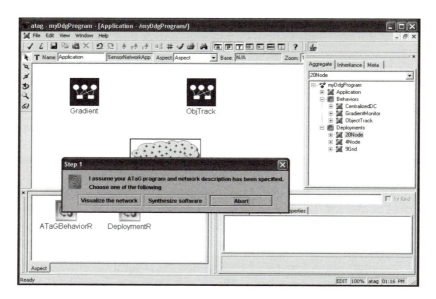

Figure 4.7   Invoking the GME model interpreters.

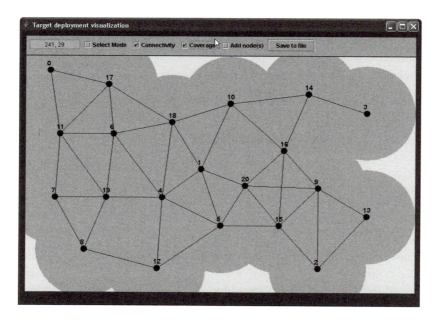

Figure 4.8   GME model interpreter: Network visualization.

```
package atag.application;

import atag.runtime.*;
import atag.sensor.*;
import atag.runtime.config.*;
import visualizer.*;

public class SampleAndThreshold implements Runnable {
        private DataPool m_dataPool;
        private DataItem m_dataitem;
        private Config m_myState;
        private Sensor m_aSensor;
        private NetworkArchitecture m_networkArchitecture;
        private GUI m_GUI;
        private GUIMessage m_guiMessage;

        public SampleAndThreshold(DataPool dp, Config myconfig,
                NetworkArchitecture t_networkArchitecture,
                GUI t_GUI) {
            m_dataPool = dp;
            m_myState = myconfig;
            m_networkArchitecture = t_networkArchitecture;
            m_GUI = t_GUI;
        }

        public void run() {
            try {
                    for(;;) {
                            /* Write output data items */
                            Thread.sleep(1000);
                    } //end for
            }
            catch (InterruptedException e) {
                    return;
            }
        }
}
```

Figure 4.9   Automatically generated skeleton code for an abstract task.

4.4.3 The ATaG simulator

To allow the application developer to test the application behavior in a simulated sensor network, a single-machine simulation and visualization mechanism was developed for ATaG. The simulation occurs in a decentralized manner with no global synchronization between the simulated nodes. A method of sending messages to the graphical visualization interface is provided to

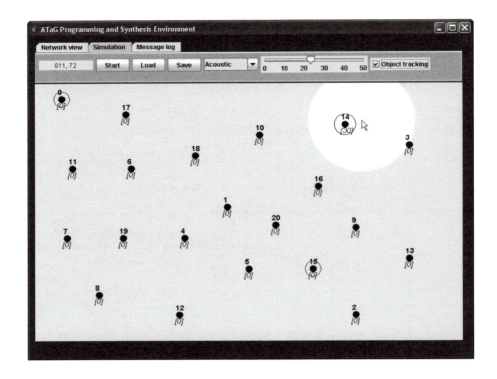

Figure 4.10   A screenshot of the simulation and visualization interface.

the application developer and can be used to perform message logging at the application (i.e., the user task) level.

Figure 4.10 is a screenshot of the simulation control and visualization interface. The application being simulated in this example is object tracking and gradient monitoring on a 20-node network. This application is discussed in detail in the next section.

4.4.4   Initialization

The current implementation of DART is designed to work with the single-machine simulation environment. Specifically, the simulation is started by launching an independent Java process for each simulated node in the network. For instance, in a 20-node network, twenty instances of DART (with different command-line arguments) will be started on the same machine.

```
package visualizer;

public class Constants {
    // The main simulation GUI is listening on this port.  Any
    // transmissions from
    // the simulation to the GUI should be sent to this socket on the
    // local machine.
    //
  public static final int VIZ_PORT = 4000;
    //
    // This socket is used by a Sensor.java instance to listen to
    // sensor readings controlled by sliders in the GUI.  When the
    // sensor is initialized, it opens a listener at the base port
    // number plus its node ID.  When a message is incoming on this
    // socket, the current reading is changed; otherwise the
    // current/old reading is returned to whoever calls
    // getReading().  Initial // value should be provided to the
    // sensor class.
    //
  public static final int ACOUSTIC_SENSOR_READINGS_BASE_PORT = 6100;
  public static final int TEMPERATURE_SENSOR_READINGS_BASE_PORT = 6200;

    //
    // This socket (base+id) is used by a node to listen for
    // messages over the
    // simulated network (from other nodes).
    //
  public static final int NODE_PROCESS_BASE_PORT = 6300;

  public static final int MIN_READING = 0;
  public static final int MAX_READING = 50;

  public static final int TEMPERATURE_SENSOR = 0;
  public static final int DEFAULT_TEMPERATURE = 0;
  public static final int ACOUSTIC_SENSOR = 1;
  public static final int DEFAULT_ACOUSTIC = 0;
}
```

Figure 4.11 Constants defined for simulation and visualization.

4.4.4.1 *Situatedness* As each DART process initializes (i.e., runs the main function of the Startup class), it reads its own 'situatedness' information from a config file that is generated automatically by the compiler and passed as a command-line parameter to the process. The config file includes information such as the node's ID, the number of tasks and data items mapped onto that node, the IDs of tasks assigned to that particular node, and the hop-scope and distance-scope parameters that are used to initialize the NetworkArchitecture module. The role of the hop-scope and distance-scope parameters was discussed in Section 3.3.6.

The simulation takes place on a single machine and all processes are assigned socket IDs on the localhost. A class `Constants` (Figure 4.11) contains basic information such as the base port number that is used by nodes to determine the suitable destination socket number for other nodes in the network.

4.4.4.2 Network interface
After the configuration information is read from file, the `NetworkStack` is initialized. The network stack determines its own port number by adding its node ID to the base port from the `Constants` class and starts a receiver thread to listen to messages on that port. Next, the network stack pings the port numbers for all other nodes in the network and waits until it can successfully communicate with all nodes. This is because each DART instance is launched independently and different receiver threads come online at different (and unpredictable) times. If the network stack of each node waits until it can contact all other nodes before returning control to the main startup routine, it ensures that if internode communication is required as part of the startup process of other modules, the messages can be sent successfully to an active receiver.

4.4.4.3 Network architecture
The startup routine for the `Network-Architecture` module reads the entire network topology information from a file that is provided as a command line parameter to the DART process. This information includes the number of nodes in the network, the X and Y range of the virtual 2D topology the nodes are situated in, the radio range and sensing range for each node, and, finally, the X and Y coordinates of each node. We assume that radio range and sensing range are the same for all nodes. We also assume that two nodes within radio range can communicate with each other, and therefore the information in the network topology file is sufficient to construct the connectivity graph for the sensor network.

In future DART versions, the `NetworkArchitecture` module will not read the topology from file. Instead, it will launch protocols that will communicate only with its neighboring nodes and simulate the gathering of local topology based on the hop-scope and distance-scope specifications. When these protocols are launched, they will (correctly) assume that the network stack has already been initialized.

4.4.4.4 Sensor interface
The simulation version of DART has a modified sensor interface. Some of the functions of the modified `Sensor` class are shown in Figure 4.13. When an application calls the `reading()` method of the `Sensor` class, it should read the latest value of the sensor. A default value is assigned to each sensor type (representing a quiescent environment for that

```
public synchronized void transmitData(
                    DataItem t_dataItem, int destinationID)
{
  Socket socket = null;
  int attempt;
  // Translate node ID into port number
  int port = Constants.NODE_PROCESS_BASE_PORT + destinationID;

  // Try to send the packet twice; if it fails, give up
  for (attempt = 0; attempt < 2; attempt++) {
    try {
      socket = new Socket("localhost", port);
      break;
    }
    catch (UnknownHostException ex) {
      System.out.println("Unknown host exception when
                  connecting to target node");
      return;
    }
    catch (IOException ex) {
      System.out.println("Attempt " + attempt + ": Node " +
                  destinationID + " not initialized");
      try {
        Thread.sleep(500);
      }
      catch (InterruptedException e) {
        System.out.println("Sleep interrupted.");
      }
    }
  }
  if (attempt == 2) {
    System.err.println("Could not connect to target node.
            Abandoning attempt.");
    return;
  }

  try {
    ObjectOutputStream oos =
                new ObjectOutputStream(socket.getOutputStream());
    oos.writeObject(t_dataItem);
    oos.flush();
    oos.close();
    socket.close();
  } catch (IOException ex1) {
    System.out.println("Trouble writing object output stream
                of data item to target node.  Giving up");
    return;
  }
}
```

Figure 4.12   transmitData() function of the Transmitter class.

```
public Sensor(int nodeID, int type) {
  myID = nodeID;
  m_type = type;
  m_value = (m_type==Constants.ACOUSTIC_SENSOR) ?
                Constants.DEFAULT_ACOUSTIC :
                Constants.DEFAULT_TEMPERATURE;
  //showSlider();
  m_receiver = new FilePoller(nodeID, this);
  m_receiverThread = new Thread(m_receiver);
  m_receiverThread.start();
}

public void setReading(int r) {
  // Changing sensor value to r
  m_value = r;
}

public int type() {
  return m_type;
}

public int reading() {
  return m_value;
}
```

Figure 4.13 The modified Sensor class for ATaG simulation.

sensor interface), and the user can manipulate the sensor readings at selected sensor nodes by a simple slider mechanism in the visualization GUI.

The visualization interface allows direct manipulation of the the values of the virtual sensor readings through the slider bar shown in the figure. Two types of sensor interfaces—acoustic and temperature—are currently supported and the value of each of them can be independently varied for each node. The screenshot of Figure 4.10 shows the values of the acoustic sensors at each node as bracketed integers below the circle representing the node.

When a sensor is initialized, the constructor launches a file poller thread. This thread periodically polls a predetermined location on the disk. The frequency of polling is configurable, and so is the on-disk rendezvous file. When the user changes the value of a sensor from the visualization GUI, the updated value is reflected in the corresponding on-disk file and is propagated to the suitable node when its file poller thread reads the value next.

Another mechanism for communicating sensor values between the visualization GUI and the simulated sensor node processes is available in the DART implementation but not enabled by default. This alternate mechanism uses a listener thread that opens a predetermined socket on the local machine. If the user changes the sensor reading through the GUI, the GUI process sends

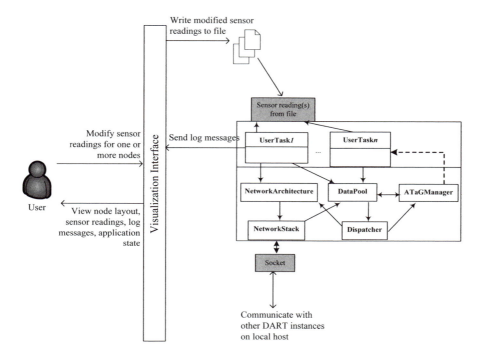

Figure 4.14   An overview of the ATaG simulator.

a message to the suitable port number. The reason for choosing the file-based communication mechanism over the socket-based one is that the former proved to be more robust in our testing than the latter, which was prone to delays and timeouts depending on the frequency of manipulation of the sensor readings through the GUI, the processing speed and memory available in the machine hosting the simulations, etc.

Note that the file-based exchange means that changes made through the GUI are not reflected immediately in the simulated sensor node. If the sensor network application calls the reading() method of its sensor class before the file poller has read the latest value from file, it could read a stale reading. This delay can be minimized by increasing the frequency of polling, but the functionality of the sensor network application typically does not (and should not) change if the reading is reflected in the simulated node with a slight delay from the time it is changed by the GUI user.

An object tracking mode is also supported for the acoustic sensor. When the object tracking mode is activated, the movement of the cursor simulates the movement of the object. Readings of acoustic sensors on sensor nodes within a certain range of the object (cursor) position are automatically adjusted in inverse proportion to the distance of the target from the node. Any such manipulation of the acoustic or temperature sensor reading through the graphical interface is reflected in the file that will be read by the sensor module when it is next sampled by one of the tasks on the simulated node.

Note that the component-based design of DART insulates other components of the system from the modified implementations of the network stack, the network architecture module, the sensor interface that reads values from files, etc. The behavior of the core modules such as the data pool, the ATaG manager, the dispatcher, etc., is not affected by the fact that the processes are communicating through sockets on the same machine, reading topology from file, etc., and not running in a real sensor network deployment.

4.4.5   Visualizing synthesized application behavior

The purpose of designing this graphical interface is to be able to evaluate the functionality of the distributed software system that is generated from the GME-based ATaG programming interface. The application-level tasks and other DART components communicate with the visualization interface so that phenomena of interest at the application level or system level can be observed. For instance, the circle around node 14 in the screenshot of Figure 4.10 indicates that the node (which is nearest to the cursor/object) has elected itself the leader and "acquired" the object in accordance with the ATaG program for object tracking. Similarly, nodes 0 and 15 have detected a temperature gradient anomaly and reported the same to the root node. The readings shown below the sensor nodes in this screenshot are zero because the acoustic readings are being displayed and not the temperature readings.

DART components can also send messages to this interface, which are displayed in the message log pane. A special class mGUI is provided to the application developer. Any messages sent to this class will be reflected in the message log pane of the visualization interface. The mGUI class, as shown in Figure 4.15, is just a wrapper around the NetworkStack and invokes a special method of the network stack that transmits the message to the GUI port and not to ports corresponding to the listener threads of other simulated sensor nodes.

When the send() method of mGUI is invoked by the user task, the message is passed onto the network stack, which in turn passes it on to the transmitGUIMessage() method of the Transmitter class that is encapsulated within the network stack module.

```
package atag.runtime;

import visualizer.*;
import atag.runtime.*;

public class mGUI {
  private NetworkStack m_networkStack;

  public mGUI(NetworkStack t_networkStack) {
    m_networkStack = t_networkStack;
  }

  // Act as a wrapper for the transmitGUIMessage method of the
  // Transmitter class, which is accessed through the
  // sendGUIMessage of the NetworkStack class
  public synchronized void send(GUIMessage msg) {
    m_networkStack.sendGUIMessage(msg);
  }
}
```

Figure 4.15   The mGUI class.

As shown in Figure 4.16, the Transmitter determines the port number for the visualization GUI from the Constants class (Figure 4.11) and makes a configurable number of attempts to send the message. The reason for having a time-out mechanism after multiple attempts is that there is a possibility that the visualization process may not be launched prior to the start of simulation. Currently, the user is expected to ensure that the visualization class is started before the multiple DART processes are fired. In case the former step is omitted, any attempts to send a message to the GUI from the individual node will fail after a predetermined number of attempts.

The visualization GUI will need to be customized to display the events of interest in a particular application. Since the semantics of each application and the events that occur therein are different, the GUI cannot incorporate a "universal" mechanism to represent high-level event abstractions. For instance, a temperature gradient monitoring application might wish to display nodes that have a high temperature in a particular color. An object tracking application might wish to display the node nearest to the object in a particular manner, or perhaps triangulate the readings from different nodes and display the estimated position of the target itself. Such customizations must be made by directly modifying the current version of the visualization classes.

Each time the application level task wants to send a message to the GUI, it instantiates and populates an instance of the GUIMessage class in the visualizer package. This class acts as the link between the application

```
public synchronized void transmitGUIMessage(GUIMessage msg) {
  // Attempt to send message to the GUI
  Socket socket = null;
  int attempt = 0;
  // GUI port is defined in the Constants class
  int port = Constants.VIZ_PORT;

  // Make two attempts to contact the GUI port;
  // sleep for 500ms between the attempts. This is configurable
  for (attempt = 0; attempt < 2; attempt++) {
    try {
      socket = new Socket("localhost", port);
      break;
    }
    catch (UnknownHostException ex) {
      System.out.println("Unknown host exception when connecting
                to GUI receiver");
      return;
    }
    catch (IOException ex) {
      System.out.println("Attempt " + attempt +
                           ": GUI not initialized");
      try {
        Thread.sleep(500);
      }
      catch (InterruptedException e) {
        System.out.println("Sleep interrupted.");
      }
    }
  }
  if (attempt == 2) {
    System.err.println("Could not connect to GUI receiver.
                Abandoning attempt.");
    return;
  }

  try {
    ObjectOutputStream viz_oos = new
                ObjectOutputStream(socket.getOutputStream());
    viz_oos.writeObject(msg);
    viz_oos.flush();
    viz_oos.close();
    socket.close();
  } catch (IOException ex1) {
    System.out.println("Trouble writing to output object stream
                or closing socket. Giving up.");
    return;
  }
}
```

Figure 4.16 sendGUIMessage() function of the Transmitter class.

and the GUI and should be modified if new types of messages or new information for existing message types is to be communicated. The GUI process parses the received GUIMessage and, depending on the type of the message received, responds in one of many ways such as adding the message to the

```
package visualizer;

import java.io.*;

public class GUIMessage
    implements Serializable {

  // The following constants are used to indicate which event
  // has triggered the transmission of this GUIMessage instance

  // Event: A message has been transmitted (with message stats)
  public static final int GUIM_XMIT = 0X01;
  // Event: A message has been received (with message stats)
  public static final int GUIM_RCV = 0X02;
  // Event: The node is alive and running (with node stats)
  public static final int GUIM_NODESTATE = 0X04;
  // Event: Application-level logging
  public static final int GUIM_NODEOUTPUT = 0X08;

  // These values are set for all types of GUIMessages
  // Timestamp and origin ID could be set by the Transmitter
  private int m_messageType;
  private String m_timeStamp;
  private int m_originID;

  // These values will be used if message is of type XMIT or RCV
  private int senderID;
  private int receiverID;
  private String xmitTime;
  private String rcvTime;

  // These values will be used if message is of type NODESTATE
  private int nodeID;
  private int[] nodeCoords;
  private int energyLevel;
  private int[] hostedTasks;
  private String nodeLabel;

  // These values will be used if message is of type NODEOUTPUT
  private String nodeOutput;
  ....
}
```

Figure 4.17   Inside the GUIMessage() class.

message log pane for that node, changing the color of the node in the display, drawing a circle around the node to indicate some node state of interest, etc.

The information sent as part of a GUIMessage is shown in the code listing of Figure 4.17. Additional message types and their associated variables can be easily defined by adding the corresponding code to this class.

```
public void messageReceived(GUIMessage msg) {
    int msgType = msg.messageType();
    int msgOrigin = msg.origin();
    String msgTimeStamp = msg.timeStamp();
    switch (msgType) {
      case GUIMessage.GUIM_NODEOUTPUT:
        if (msg.message().equals("LEADER")) {
            m_topograph.isLeader(msgOrigin);
        }
        if (msg.message().equals("EXLEADER")) {
            m_topograph.notLeader(msgOrigin);
        }
        if (msg.message().equals("FIRE")) {
            m_topograph.onFire(msgOrigin);
        }
        if (msg.message().equals("NOFIRE")) {
            System.err.println("Node:" + msgOrigin + " not on fire");
            m_topograph.notOnFire(msgOrigin);
        }
        if (msgOrigin == 0) {
            rootLog += msg.message() + "\n";
            rootLogArea.setText(rootLog);
        }
      case GUIMessage.GUIM_RCV:
      case GUIMessage.GUIM_XMIT:
        m_messageLogger.addLog(msgOrigin, msgTimeStamp, msg.message());
        break;
      case GUIMessage.GUIM_NODESTATE:
        break;
    }
    // If the node that sent this message is also selected
    // for visualization, update its log in 'real time'
    if (Integer.parseInt((String) idList.getSelectedItem())
                    == msgOrigin)
        messageLogArea.setText(m_messageLogger.nodeLog(msgOrigin));
}
```

Figure 4.18 Processing the messages received from sensor nodes. The `messageReceived()` function of the `MainWindow` class.

The actual visualization interface is provided by an independent Java application that includes the same `visualizer` package with DART in order to facilitate exchange of GUIMessage instances through serialization. When the visualizer receives a message from one of the simulated nodes, it determines the message type and implements the custom responses for various message types and contents. Figure 4.18 is an excerpt from the `MainWindow` class of the visualizer application. The routine shown is invoked by a listener thread that listens on a predefined port number for messages of type `GUIMessage`.

The listing shows some of the customized responses to events specific to the temperature gradient monitoring and object tracking applications. This code can be easily modified to add more behaviors, in concert with extensions to the GUIMessage class.

Our use of a GME-based graphical modeling language as a concrete syntax for an ATaG program is just one of many possible representations of the program. As mentioned earlier, this decision was influenced mainly by the ease of use of a GME-based user interface, and by the fact that we could realize a concrete syntax that corresponded very closely to the abstract syntax of an ATaG program. XML or even RDF representations of ATaG programs should be possible, provided the software synthesis tool chain is configured to read and process such representations, and that the end users have a reasonably intuitive interface to create and modify ATaG programs in these alternate representations. In fact, it should be possible to write GME model interpreters that read from and write to XML files, that are then consumed by software synthesis modules.

CHAPTER 5

CASE STUDY: APPLICATION DEVELOPMENT WITH ATaG

We now illustrate the process of ATaG programming and software synthesis through a case study. In this case study, the programmer is interested in synthesizing an application consisting of two behaviors—object tracking and temperature gradient monitoring—for a particular network deployment.

The purpose of this case study is

- to walk the reader through the complete process of translating a high-level functional description of application functionality into deployable code for each node of a target network using the ATaG programming model and application development environment,

- to illustrate the use of the graphical interface for translating abstract syntax of the ATaG program into the concrete syntax used for software synthesis,

Architecture-Independent Programming for Wireless Sensor Networks
By Amol B. Bakshi, Viktor K. Prasanna
Copyright © 2008 John Wiley & Sons, Inc.

- to discuss in detail the code to be associated with each element of the program by the programmer and the code that is automatically generated by the software synthesis tool, and

- to illustrate the architecture independence and composability of ATaG programs, which allow the process of developing ATaG program libraries to be entirely decoupled from the process of selecting and compiling a set of programs from the library onto the desired target deployment.

5.1   OVERVIEW OF THE USE CASE

5.2   DESIGNING THE MACROPROGRAMS

5.2.1   Temperature gradient monitoring

We now discuss the macroprogramming formulation in ATaG of temperature gradient monitoring functionality. An ATaG program that modeled this behavior as a neighbor-to-neighbor protocol was discussed as part of the programming idioms in Section 2.5.2. Briefly, each node periodically compares its temperature reading with the reading of its neighboring nodes. If the gradient is above a certain threshold, an alarm notification is sent to a designated root node.

There are many ways of expressing this behavior using the ATaG primitives. For instance, a simple centralized version can be defined as shown in Figure 5.1. In this approach, the sampling task on each node produces the temperature reading, and all temperature readings are transmitted to a central supervisor task running on the root node. Centralized solutions are usually undesirable in energy-constrained sensor networks because the cost of transmitting raw data to a central location and performing the processing outside the network defeats the purpose of smart sensor nodes equipped with computational capabilities to perform in-network, on-the-fly processing.

An ATaG program that uses hierarchical data collection for gradient monitoring is shown in Figure 5.2. In this approach, the TSampler task is instantiated on each node of the network. The assumption throughout this use case is that all nodes are equipped with both temperature and acoustic sensors, hence the sampler tasks can be instantiated on every single node. The TSampler produces a data item of type Temperature at each invocation. This data item simply encapsulates the temperature reading at that invocation. This data item is also added only to the local data pool as indicated by the output channel

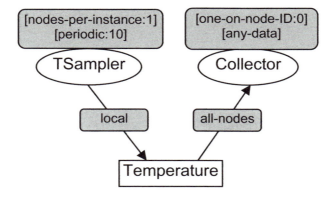

Figure 5.1 Abstract syntax: Temperature gradient monitoring using a centralized algorithm.

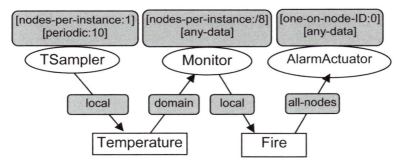

Figure 5.2 Abstract syntax: Temperature gradient monitoring using hierarchical data collection.

annotation. The actual gradient monitoring is done by the Monitor tasks. As shown in the task annotation for the Monitor task, exactly 8 of these tasks are instantiated in the network. The task placement annotation directs the compiler to divide the network into 8 virtual domains and assign one Monitor task instance to each domain. The exact placement of the Monitor task instance within each of the 8 groups is left to the compiler. The runtime system also ensures that instances of the Temperature data items that are produced on nodes within a domain are routed to the Monitor task assigned to that domain. This is indicated by the input channel annotation for the Monitor task. Finally, the supervisor task AlarmActuator is instantiated on exactly one node and monitors any alarm notifications sent by Monitor tasks.

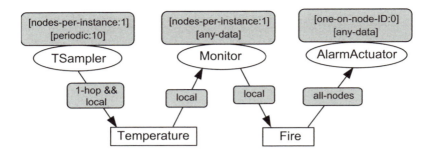

Figure 5.3   Abstract syntax: Temperature gradient monitoring through neighbor-to-neighbor interactions.

This approach represents hierarchical data collection and processing, where a three-level tree is formed in the network. At the topmost level, the supervisor task collects information about gradient violation notifications. At the middle level, exactly 8 Monitor tasks collect the data from their non-overlapping domains and determine if the gradient between neighboring nodes in their domain exceeds the prespecified threshold. At the lowest level of the tree, temperature sampler tasks at each node periodically produce the Temperature data items that contain sensor readings.

Another possible ATaG program that we implement in this use case is shown in Figure 5.3. The approach in this program is to accomplish the desired overall functionality by means of interactions between neighboring sensor nodes. The abstract tasks in this program are the same as the tasks in the hierarchical data processing approach. The TSampler task periodically samples the temperature and sends out the sampled reading to its local data pool and also to the data pools of its 1-hop neighbors. The Monitor task is also instantiated on every node in the network. This task waits for input data item of type Temperature. The output channel annotation for the TSampler task implies that the Monitor task will receive temperature readings from its own node and from its 1-hop neighbors. All readings received by the Monitor are recorded as part of its local state information. The task also continually checks the gradient between its host node and the neighboring nodes and generates an alert (Fire data item) when a gradient is exceeded. The alert is routed to the AlarmActuator task that is mapped onto a single supervisor node in the system. In this approach, each gradient violation between a pair of nodes will result in a message from the Monitor tasks on each of the two nodes to the supervisor node.

We discuss the imperative portion of this ATaG program in detail in Section 5.4.

5.2.2 Object detection and tracking

We now discuss the approaches to writing ATaG macroprograms for the object detection and tracking functionality. At the high level, the program should determine the presence of objects of interest in the sensor field at all times. We simplify the use case by assuming that identity maintenance and tracking is not a concern in this example. In other words, if one or more objects of interest are in the sensor field, the application should only generate periodic reports that indicate the presence and the approximate location of each object. The program is not required to be intelligent enough to detect if an object at some location X' at time T' is the same object as was detected at location X at an earlier time T.

As mentioned briefly in Section 2.5, a simple algorithm for object tracking [55] requires each node to periodically sample its sensing interface and compare it against a predefined threshold. A reading that exceeds the threshold is indicative of the presence of a target in the sensing range. The nodes that detect the target elect a leader node, which is the node with the maximum reading among all nodes involved in the election. The leader node then performs some processing of the set of sensor readings and transmits the resultant estimate of target location to a base station.

As in the previous example of temperature gradient monitoring, there are various approaches toward formulating this functionality in terms of an ATaG program. While the sampling task and the supervisor task are quite straightforward in terms of their logic, the implementation of the distributed leader election can be realized in multiple ways.

Figure 5.4 is an example ATaG program for this behavior. The `SampleAnd-Threshold` task is executed periodically on each node. As indicated by the task name, it samples the acoustic sensor in each invocation and produces a `TargetAlert` notification when the reading is above some threshold that is indicative of the presence of an object of interest within the sensing range of the node. All nodes that have a given target in range at any given time produce these notifications. To perform leader election, it is important for each node that has detected the target to receive notifications from every other node that has also detected the target. The `TargetAlert` notification contains some measure of the distance of the target from the node as indicated by the sensor reading, or some other mechanism that can be used to determine the criteria for the leader election. Suppose that each node sends its sensor reading as part

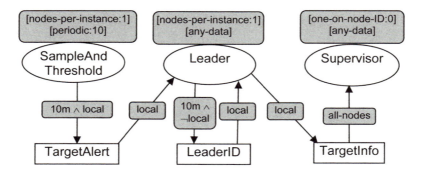

Figure 5.4   Alternate ATaG program for object tracking by local leader election.

of the `TargetAlert` and the node with the maximum reading (i.e., which is closest to the target in this sense) should elect itself the leader.

If the target can be detected at a maximum distance of d from the acoustic sensor on a particular sensor node, the maximum distance between nodes that can detect the same target is $2d$. Hence, the output channel annotation for the sampling and thresholding task should require the target alert to be sent to all nodes within distance $2d$ of the node where the alert is produced. In this example, the "10 m" label implies that the sensing radius of the acoustic sensor is 5 meters.

Now that the `TargetAlert` is disseminated from each node that has detected the object to every other node that has detected the object, it is necessary to define the mechanism of leader election in the ATaG program. In this case, we define a `Leader` task that is instantiated on each node of the network. This task consumes all `TargetAlerts` that are sent to the node from its neighboring nodes and also from the sampling task on the same node. The task maintains local state that consists of the readings received from the neighborhood. Using this information, the task can compare its own reading to the neighbor's readings; and if its own reading is the maximum, it declares itself the leader and also generates a `TargetInfo` notification to the `Supervisor` task on the root node. Now, communication in the sensor network is inherently asynchronous because the sampling of the sensor on the nodes within range of the target is unlikely to be precisely synchronized. Hence, each node will generate its `TargetAlert` at different points in time. Also, multi-hop packet transmissions could introduce other delays in transmitting the `TargetAlert`.

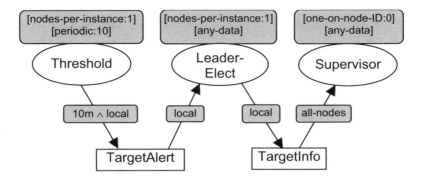

Figure 5.5   Abstract syntax: ATaG program for object tracking by local leader election.

It is desirable to avoid situations where two tasks that have detected the same target elect themselves the leader based on incomplete and different pictures of the same reality. In the sample program of Figure 5.4, the Leader task generates a LeaderID data item when it declares itself a leader—that is, at the same time that it generates the TargetInfo item. This item is sent to all the nodes that may have detected the target, and it is meant to act as a preemptive notification to other nodes that might be about to elect themselves leaders.

Naturally, this scheme could suffer from the same shortcomings as the problem it is designed to solve - i.e., the LeaderID notification could be delivered at different times to different nodes, etc. The intent here is not to propose this as a foolproof solution to the distributed leader election problem, but to illustrate how the ATaG channel annotations and other features can be used to create sophisticated distributed behaviors using a concise notation. The program shown in the figure has all the advantages of the ATaG programming model: It is architecture-independent, the tasks are decoupled from each other by defining them in terms of input and output data items, etc.

The ATaG program that we actually implement in this case study is shown in Figure 5.5 and is a slightly modified and simplified version of the earlier program. In this program, the LeaderID data item is not generated and the Leader task makes the self-election decision and generates the TargetInfo node without attempting to notify its neighborhood of the decision. The details of the imperative part of this program are discussed in Section 5.5.

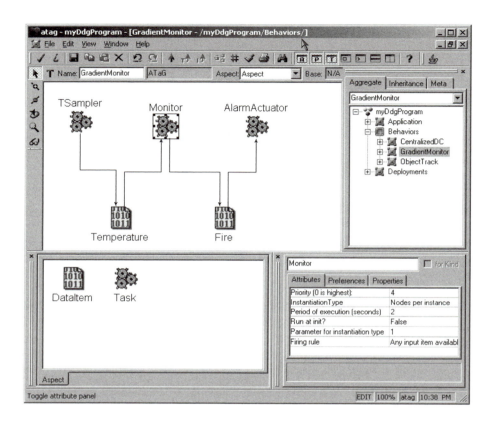

Figure 5.6 Concrete syntax: GME model of ATaG program for gradient monitoring.

5.3 SPECIFYING THE DECLARATIVE PORTION

The concrete syntax of this program as modeled in GME is shown in Figure 5.6. Note that the the concrete syntax of the declarative part of the ATaG program is identical to the abstract syntax of the task graph. The programmer directly translates the task graph into the GME model by dragging, naming, and annotating the desired number of abstract tasks, data items, and channels into the modeling window. The ease of use this engenders is perhaps the most significant advantage of visual ATaG programming through GME.

The GME model of the ATaG program for object tracking is shown in Figure 5.7. Again, the concrete syntax is identical to the abstract syntax.

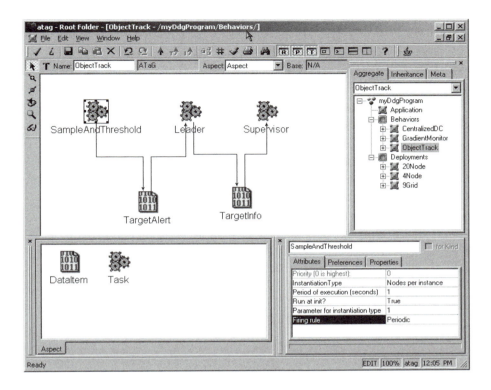

Figure 5.7   Concrete syntax: GME model of ATaG program for object tracking.

5.4 IMPERATIVE PORTION: TEMPERATURE GRADIENT MONITORING

5.4.1 Abstract data items: Temperature and fire

There are two abstract data items in the gradient monitoring program. The first data item, called `Temperature`, is used by tasks to pass the temperature readings to other tasks. Note that the nomenclature is entirely up to the application developer. In the current version of DART, management of sensing resources is entirely up to the user-level task. Tasks have to make the suitable calls to the sensing interface (e.g., the temperature sensor), and they process the reading as desired. In this case, the reading has to be sent to the neighboring nodes by adding it to the data pool. The application developer therefore names the data

```
package atag.application;

import java.io.*;

public class Temperature implements Serializable {
        private int m_temperatureReading;

        public int get() {
                return m_temperatureReading;
        }
        public void set(int temp) {
                m_temperatureReading = temp;
        }
}
```

Figure 5.8 Code associated with the Temperature data item.

```
package atag.application;

import java.io.Serializable;

public class Fire implements Serializable {
   int x = 0;
}
```

Figure 5.9 Code associated with the Fire data item.

item that will hold the temperature reading as Temperature, but the name of the data item has no mandatory relationship with it contents.

The listing for the Java class associated with the Temperature data item is shown in Figure 5.8. Definition of the member variables and methods of this class is entirely up to the programmer. Figure 5.9 shows a similar listing for the Fire data item, which is produced on a node by the Monitor task when a gradient violation is detected.

5.4.2 Abstract task: Monitor

We now focus on the imperative portion of the Monitor task. Figure 5.10 shows the code listing for the members of the Monitor class. Lines 1–20 in this case are automatically generated by the software synthesis tool that inspects the declarative part of the ATaG program for this purpose. Lines

```
1    package atag.application;
2
3    import atag.runtime.*;
4    import atag.runtime.config.*;
5    import visualizer.*;
6
7    public class Monitor implements Runnable {
8        // runtime objects
9        DataPool m_dataPool;
10       private Config m_myState;
11       private NetworkArchitecture m_networkArchitecture;
12
13       // visualization and logging
14       private mGUI m_GUI;
15       private GUIMessage m_guiMessage;
16
17       // input and output data items
18       private Fire m_fire = null;
19       private Temperature m_temperature = null;
20
21       // local state variables
22       private static int myReading = 0;
23       private static boolean wasOnFire = false, isOnFire = false;
24       private static int[] targetReadings;
25       private static int[] neighborIDs;
26       private static int[][] neighborCoords;
27
28       ....
29   }
```

Figure 5.10   Members of the Monitor class.

21–26 are specific to the business logic of the task and are added by the programmer as part of populating the code skeleton.

User-level tasks are part of the atag.application package in the current version of DART. The import statements in lines 3–5 allow the user task to access other modules. The atag.runtime package provides access to the data pool class which implements the get() and put() calls for consuming and producing data items, respectively. The second module of this package that is useful to the application-level task is the NetworkArchitecture. As explained in Section 3.3.6, this module is in charge of maintaining the neighborhood information to an extent determined by the channel annotations of the task hosted on that node. For instance, if a task on that node has an input channel that gathers data items from a 1-hop neighborhood, it is natural to assume that the task may want to know the constitution of the neighborhood in terms of the number of nodes and the location of each node in that neighborhood. The `NetworkArchitecture` class maintains this information and furnishes it to the task on request.

The `atag.runtime.config` package is imported because it includes the `Config` class. This class contains state information for the node such as its own ID, its location in some real or virtual coordinate system (if relevant in that particular deployment), the label of the node (if any), etc. When a user-level task initializes, it uses the `Config` class to determine where it is placed in the network. Lines 9–12 in Figure 5.10 show these classes being instantiated in the `Monitor` class.

The `mGUI` and `GUIMessage` classes of lines 14 and 15 are used by the task to send messages to the visualization environment. These classes are basically wrappers around the transmit call of the network stack and cause the message to be sent to a specific port number on the local host that is monitored by the visualization process.

`Fire` and `Temperature` are user-defined abstract data items in the ATaG program for gradient monitoring. The software synthesis tools determines that these two data items are associated with this task through output and input channels and creates placeholder instantiations in the class skeleton. The end user is free to delete these instantiations, create additional instantiations, or instantiate these in a different place in the code as desired.

Lines 22–26 are the class members that are part of the task-specific semantics. In the ATaG model, as in most data-driven programming models, the data pool is the only persistent global storage that is accessed by tasks on different nodes and at different times. The DART runtime system has no provision for allocating and managing memory space for individual tasks. If a task is to maintain some information across invocations, such information is to be stored in static variables as shown in this example. This approach is suitable for the current ATaG implementation because there is no support for task migration, and hence preserving the task state across nodes is not a concern. The arrays in lines 25 and 26 are used to store the IDs of the neighboring nodes and their x and y coordinates. The actual temperature readings received from the nodes are stored in the `targetReadings` array (line 24). When a data item produced by a task on one node is transmitted for consumption to another node, the runtime system automatically tags it with the time and location it was produced. The task can associate data items with the individual nodes in its neighborhood by means of this information in the data item and the neighborhood information from the network architecture module.

```
 1    . . .
 2
 3    public Monitor(DataPool dp, Config myconfig,
 4                   NetworkArchitecture t_networkArchitecture,
 5                   mGUI t_GUI) {
 6        m_dataPool = dp;
 7        m_myState = myconfig;
 8        m_GUI = t_GUI;
 9        m_networkArchitecture = t_networkArchitecture;
10        neighborIDs = m_networkArchitecture.kHopNeighborIDs(1);
11        neighborCoords = m_networkArchitecture.kHopNeighborCoords(1);
12        targetReadings = new int[neighborIDs.length];
13    }
14
15    private void setNeighborReading(int nid, int d) {
16        for (int i = 0; i < neighborIDs.length; i++)
17            if (neighborIDs[i] == nid)
18                targetReadings[i] = d;
19    }
20
21    private int getNeighborReading(int nid) {
22        for (int i = 0; i < neighborIDs.length; i++)
23            if (neighborIDs[i] == nid)
24                return targetReadings[i];
25        return -1;
26    }
27
28    private void log(String msg) {
29        m_guiMessage = new GUIMessage(m_myState.myID(),
30                                      GUIMessage.GUIM_NODEOUTPUT, "");
31        m_guiMessage.setNodeOutput(msg);
32        m_GUI.send(m_guiMessage);
33    }
34
35    . . .
```

Figure 5.11 Constructor and helper functions of the `Monitor` class.

Figure 5.11 shows the constructor and some user-defined helper functions for the class. A skeleton for the class constructor is automatically generated by the software synthesis tool. Lines 3–9 are applicable to all abstract tasks and are not specific to a particular application logic. This section instantiates the handles to the data pool, the configuration (state) information for the node, a handle to the visualization interface, and to the network architecture module. In this example, since the monitor task will need to determine and then record readings from its neighborhood, the programmer has added the statements in lines 10–12 to obtain this information from the network architecture module and to create an array to store readings from each neighbor. In the current DART prototype, the network architecture module does not really run a topology creation and maintenance protocol but simply reads the information from a file on the local disk. The topology or the connectivity of the network does not change at runtime. Hence, this information can be collected as part of the class constructor. If the target deployment is such that the constitution of the neighborhood could keep changing, a suitable re-coding will be required to anticipate the possibility that the result of a call to the kHopNeighborIDs and kHopNeighborCoords functions of the NetworkArchitecture could change between invocations.

The getNeighborReading and setNeighborReading functions are helper functions defined by the programmer. These functions simplify access to the integer array where readings are stored, and they are not related to the data pool or the network stack. The log function is another user-defined function that is used to send messages to the visualization interface.

The main function that is executed each time an instance of this abstract task is invoked is shown in Figure 5.12. Each task has to implement the run() function because application tasks implement the Runnable interface, which defines this function. Implementing the Runnable interface effectively makes the abstract task instance a thread that can be invoked by the AtagManager when its firing conditions are met. We now examine the run function of this task in more detail.

At the high level, the purpose of this task is to continually read the temperature readings produced on its own nodes and sent by its neighboring nodes and, whenever such a reading is received, calculate the difference between the local reading and each of the neighbors to determine if a prespecified threshold is exceeded. If this threshold is exceeded, the task should produce an alarm notification in the form of a data item of type Fire. The name of this data item is chosen as an indication of a possible event that could have occurred, it is not necessary that each gradient violation necessarily indicates a fire, and the programmer is free to choose any other preferred name.

When the task is executed, it first reads a data item of type Temperature from the data pool. This call is guaranteed to succeed because this task has only one input data item and it is scheduled for execution only when the data item is produced. ATaG semantics ensure that each invocation of this call results in a valid (non-null) result.

The parameters to the getData() call are the IDs of the task requesting the data item and the ID of the data item being requested. The ID of the task is required in order to ensure that each task can consume each data item only once. For a more detailed rationale, see Section 2.4.4. The IDConstants class is generated automatically during code synthesis as part

```
1    public void run() {
2        DataItem t_dataItem = m_dataPool.getData(
3                        IDConstants.T_MONITOR,
4                        IDConstants.D_TEMPERATURE);
5        if (t_dataItem == null)
6            return;
7        isOnFire = false;
8        m_temperature = (Temperature) t_dataItem.core();
9        int senderID = t_dataItem.originID();
10       if (senderID == m_myState.myID()) {
11           myReading = m_temperature.get();
12       } else {
13           setNeighborReading(senderID, m_temperature.get());
14       }
15
16       for (int n = 0; n < neighborIDs.length; n++) {
17           if (getNeighborReading(neighborIDs[n]) != -1) {
18               if (myReading - getNeighborReading(neighborIDs[n])
19                                                       > 5) {
20                   isOnFire = true;
21                   break;
22               }
23           }
24       }
25       if (isOnFire && !wasOnFire) {
26           m_fire = new Fire();
27           DataItem m_dataitem = new DataItem(
28                        IDConstants.D_FIRE,
29                        IDConstants.T_MONITOR, m_fire);
30           m_dataPool.putData(m_dataitem);
31           log("FIRE");
32       } else if (!isOnFire && wasOnFire) {
33           m_fire = new Fire();
34           DataItem m_dataitem = new DataItem(
35                        IDConstants.D_FIRE,
36                        IDConstants.T_MONITOR, m_fire);
37           m_dataPool.putData(m_dataitem);
38           log("NOFIRE");
39       }
40       wasOnFire = isOnFire;
41   }
```

Figure 5.12   The main function of the `Monitor` task.

of the `atag.application` package. This class contains a list of constants corresponding to the names of the tasks and data items. For instance, if an abstract task `Monitor` is present in the program, a corresponding integer constant T_MONITOR is generated, where the T_ denotes a task. The constants act as unique identifiers for the tasks and data items. The runtime system uses these unique integer identifiers instead of the names of the tasks. The application developer who writes the code for abstract tasks can then use only the names of the constants and not integer identifiers that will change depending on the number of data items and tasks in the program. This provides a degree of portability.

The isOnFire flag is used to determine if an alarm condition exists. At each execution of the task, this flag is initially set to false (line 7). In line 8, the program extracts the actual data structure corresponding to the Temperature abstract data item. Note that the call to getData() in line 2 returns an object of type DataItem, not of type Temperature. The DataItem class is a wrapper for the user-defined abstract data item class and contains additional such as the location and time of origin of that data item. To access the actual data structure, it is necessary to invoke the core() method of the DataItem class. The temperature is then stored in the m_temperature class, and the ID of the originating node is determined in line 9. If the data item originates on the same node, the temperature reading is stored as myReading; otherwise it is assigned to a suitable location in the array that records readings received from neighbors. Line 10 demonstrates the use of the m_myState instance of the Config class. In this example, the task uses the config information to determine the ID of the node it is hosted on. In lines 16–24, the node's own reading is checked against each of its neighbors to see if it exceeds the threshold of 5 units, and the isOnFire flag is set to true if such a situation is encountered.

In this example, we decided to use the Fire data item (which is supposed to indicate an alarm condition) in a slightly different way. For instance, the alarm can be sounded each time the gradient violation is detected. However, consider a case where the gradient rises above the threshold and stays that way for multiple sampling periods. Instead of producing the alarm at each sampling period and thereby wasting communication and computation resources, we chose to produce the alarm condition only at the transition between a "fire" state and a "no-fire" state.

As shown in lines 26–30, the process of producing a data item involves instantiating the corresponding class (Fire), wrapping it within a DataItem class, and then adding the DataItem class (and not the original Fire class) to the data pool through the putdata() call. During the transition between states, a corresponding log message is also produced for transmission to the visualization interface. When such application-specific messages are received, the visualization can be customized to denote the event graphically; in our case, we highlight that node during the transition from no-fire to fire and retain the highlighting until the next transition message is received.

```
1   package atag.application;
2
3   import atag.runtime.*;
4   import atag.sensor.*;
5   import atag.runtime.config.*;
6   import visualizer.*;
7
8   public class TSampler implements Runnable {
9     private Temperature m_temperature = new Temperature();
10    private DataPool m_dataPool;
11    private DataItem m_dataitem;
12    private Config m_myState;
13    private Sensor m_tSensor;
14    private mGUI m_GUI;
15    private GUIMessage m_guiMessage;
16
17    private static int lastReading = Constants.DEFAULT_TEMPERATURE;
18
19    public TSampler(DataPool dp, Config myconfig,
20                    NetworkArchitecture t_networkArchitecture,
21                    mGUI t_GUI) {
22      m_tSensor = new Sensor(myconfig.myID(),
23                             Constants.TEMPERATURE_SENSOR);
24      m_dataPool = dp;
25      m_myState = myconfig;
26      m_GUI = t_GUI;
27    }
28
29    private void log(String msg) {
30      m_guiMessage = new GUIMessage(m_myState.myID(),
31                             GUIMessage.GUIM_NODEOUTPUT, "");
32      m_guiMessage.setNodeOutput(msg);
33      m_GUI.send(m_guiMessage);
34    }
35    ...
36  }
```

Figure 5.13 Constructor and members of the TSampler class.

5.4.3   Abstract task: Temperature sampler

We now discuss the imperative portion of the TSampler task. The code listing
for the constructor and members of the Java class is is Figure 5.13, and the
main function (run()) is listed in Figure 5.14.

Lines 1–6 in Figure 5.13 import the packages necessary for the application
level task to be able to access other classes in the runtime, the visualization
interface, and the sensor interface. In the current version of DART, the sensor

```
1
2    public void run() {
3      try {
4        for (; ; ) {
5          int reading = m_tSensor.reading();
6          if (reading != lastReading) {
7            m_dataitem = new DataItem(
8                          IDConstants.D_TEMPERATURE,
9                          IDConstants.T_TSAMPLER, m_temperature);
10           m_temperature.set(reading);
11           m_dataPool.putData(m_dataitem);
12           lastReading = reading;
13           }
14         Thread.sleep(5000);
15       }
16     }
17     catch (InterruptedException e) {
18       return;
19     }
20   }
```

Figure 5.14   Main function of the TSampler class.

interface is modeled as an instance of the Sensor class. The instantiation of a Sensor class to access the temperature sensor is shown in line 13. The details of the sensor interface class were discussed in Section 4.4.4.4.

The temperature sampler task wishes to access the temperature sensor. Hence, the suitable constant TEMPERATURE_SENSOR is passed to the constructor of the sensor class (lines 22–23). The log() function (lines 29–34) is defined here by the programmer as a convenient way of sending messages to the visualization front end.

The run() function of this class, as shown in Figure 5.14, is quite straightforward. The TSampler task is annotated in the declarative part of the ATaG program as a task with a periodic firing rule and a period of 5 seconds. At node initialization, the ATaGManager invokes the run() function of all periodic tasks that are marked run-at-init by the programmer. The actual periodic execution is performed in the infinite for loop (lines 4–19) in the task itself. The for loop is automatically generated as part of software synthesis, and the programmer has to fill in the actual computation that will be performed at each periodic invocation of the task.

In a naive implementation, the sampler task will produce a Temperature data item at each invocation. However, if the temperature is unchanged between invocations, this approach will result in a lot of unnecessary computation and communication (to 1-hop neighbors). Hence, the sampler task only produces a temperature data item when a change is detected between the temperature reading at the last invocation and the reading at the current invocation. In line 5, the task samples the temperature sensor. Then the reading is compared with the last reading stored in the local static variable of lastReading. If the two are not the same, a new data item of type Temperature is created and added to the data pool (lines 7–11).

Note that this task is not aware of how the output reading is processed. Since ATaG is a data-driven model, the sampler task is defined entirely in terms of its input and output data items – in this case, the output data item of the Temperature. The imperative portion of the task does not invoke any other application-level tasks. Its only concern is to produce a data item of the Temperature type and add it to the data pool when some condition is met—in this case, when the current temperature reading is different from the reading in the previous invocation. The annotation on the output channel corresponding to this data type, along with the presence of a task that is dependent on the Temperature data item as one of its inputs, drives further computation and communication in the application.

5.4.4   Abstract task: Alarm actuator

We now discuss the imperative portion of the AlarmActuator task. The complete code listing for the Java class corresponding to this task is shown in Figure 5.15.

The declarative part of this ATaG program requires this task to be hosted on a root node with a fixed node ID, say, zero. This node will typically correspond to a supervisor station. All data items of type Fire will be routed to this node per the ATaG specification. The data item of type Fire is produced by the Monitor task only when a temperature gradient that exceeds the prespecified threshold is detected. Hence, a receipt of this data item at the supervisor nodes indicates that an abnormal condition exists somewhere in the sensor network. When the Monitor task produces the data item on a particular node where the abnormality is detected, it does not explicitly add the node information to the data item. However, the DART runtime system tags each data item with the location and time of its production.

The functionality in lines 1–20 of Figure 5.15 has been discussed earlier for other abstract tasks. The run() method of the AlarmActuator is straightforward. This method is invoked whenever an instance of type Fire is added to the data pool of the node that hosts this abstract task—that is, the supervisor node. The semantics of any-data firing rule guarantee that whenever the run() method is invoked, a data item of type Fire exists in the data pool and the call to getData() in line 22 never returns null. The check for a null return

```
1    package atag.application;
2
3    import atag.runtime.*;
4    import atag.runtime.config.*;
5    import visualizer.*;
6
7    public class AlarmActuator implements Runnable {
8      DataPool m_dataPool;
9      private Config m_myState;
10     private mGUI m_GUI;
11     private GUIMessage m_guiMessage;
12
13     public AlarmActuator(DataPool dp, Config myconfig,
14                     NetworkArchitecture t_networkArchitecture,
15                     mGUI t_GUI) {
16       m_dataPool = dp;
17       m_myState = myconfig;
18       m_GUI = t_GUI;
19     }
20
21     public void run() {
22       DataItem t_dataItem = m_dataPool.getData(
23                           IDConstants.T_ALARMACTUATOR,
24                           IDConstants.D_FIRE);
25       Fire t_fire = null;
26       if (t_dataItem != null) {
27         t_fire = (Fire) t_dataItem.core();
28         int nodeOnFire = t_dataItem.originID();
29         m_guiMessage = new GUIMessage(m_myState.myID(),
30                               GUIMessage.GUIM_NODEOUTPUT, "");
31         m_guiMessage.setNodeOutput("Node " + nodeOnFire +
32                               " is ON FIRE!");
33         m_GUI.send(m_guiMessage);
34       }
35     }
36   }
```

Figure 5.15   Complete code listing for the AlarmActuator task.

value in line 26 is added as a precautionary measure to detect the correctness of the implementation of the data pool manager.

When the data item is retrieved from the pool, its origin ID is determined by a call to originID() of the data item. Note that this method is supported by the DataItem class and not by any application-specific data item such as Fire. The origin information is automatically added to the data item in the DART runtime. Currently, the only result of receiving the data item is a notification to the visualization interface. The ID of the node "on fire" is passed to the

```
1    package atag.application;
2    import java.io.Serializable;
3
4    public class TargetAlert implements Serializable {
5
6      private int m_targetDistance;
7      private boolean acquired;
8
9      public void setAcquired(boolean flag) {
10        acquired = flag;
11     }
12
13     public boolean acquired() {
14        return acquired;
15     }
16
17     public void setDistance(int d) {
18        m_targetDistance = d;
19     }
20
21     public int distance() {
22        return m_targetDistance;
23     }
24
25   }
```

Figure 5.16   Code listing for the TargetAlert data item.

graphical front end, which then highlights the node in a system-wide map of the deployment.

5.5 IMPERATIVE PORTION: OBJECT DETECTION AND TRACKING

5.5.1 Abstract data items: TargetAlert and TargetInfo

There are two types of data items in the ATaG program for object detection and tracking. The TargetAlert data item is produced by the sampler task whenever the reading of the acoustic sensor is above a certain threshold. This data item indicates that an object of interest has been detected in the vicinity of the node where this data item is produced. The code listing for the corresponding class is shown in Figure 5.16. This data item has two variables; one corresponding to the distance of the target from this node (line 6) and the other indicating whether this data item corresponds to the acquisition of a target or

```
1   package atag.application;
2   import java.io.Serializable;
3
4   public class TargetInfo implements Serializable {
5
6     private int[] myCoords;
7     private int reportingNode;
8
9     public TargetInfo(int[] myc, int nodeid) {
10      myCoords = myc;
11      reportingNode = nodeid;
12    }
13
14    public int reportingNode() {
15      return reportingNode;
16    }
17    public int[] coords() {
18      return myCoords;
19    }
20    public int yCoords() {
21      return myCoords[1];
22    }
23    public int xCoord() {
24      return myCoords[0];
25    }
26  }
```

Figure 5.17   Code listing for the TargetInfo data item.

the loss of an acquired target. The reason for producing a TargetAlert data item corresponding to the loss of an acquired target is discussed in later sections. A set of helper methods are also defined for the abstract task to read and modify the values in this data item.

The TargetInfo data item (Figure 5.17) is produced by the Leader and sent to the Supervisor task. Ideally, only one of the nodes from among the set of nodes that has detected the target at any given point in time sends an instance of the TargetInfo data item to the Supervisor. This data item could contain information about the location of the data item. For instance, based on the locations of the nodes producing the TargetAlert data item, along with the distance readings estimated by each node from the target, the Leader task could compute the position of the target in some coordinate system. The details of distance estimation and triangulation will depend heavily on the parameters of the sensing interface and are outside the scope of this illustrative example. The variable myCoords is a placeholder for the target coordinates and is not actually used in this ATaG program. The only parameter of interest in the current implementation is the ID of the reporting node. Note that this information can also be extracted from the DataItem class by invoking the suitable method. In this example, we also store this information as part of the application-level abstract data item. As shown in the code listing, a set of helper methods are defined for this class.

5.5.2   Abstract Task: SampleAndThreshold

Figure 5.18 shows the complete code listing for the SampleAndThreshold task in the object detection and tracking application. The purpose of this task is similar to the TSampler class of the temperature gradient monitoring application. Similar to the temperature sampler, this task is executed periodically with the period of execution specified in the declarative part of the program. At each invocation, the task samples the acoustic sensor and possibly produces a TargetAlert data item, depending on the value of the sensor reading.

In this case study, we record the sensor reading in the variable reserved for transmitting the distance of the object from the local node. As shown in lines 35–53, the imperative portion of this task is quite simple. At each (periodic) invocation, the acoustic sensor is sampled and the reading is stored in the latestReading variable. If the current reading is greater than zero, it means that the object is within sensing range of this node. We assume that a quiescent environment corresponds to a zero reading at the sensor and any nonzero reading indicates the presence of the object of interest. The target alert is produced and added to the local data pool. The acquired flags is also set to true if it is not already set. If the current reading is zero, there are two possibilities. Either the node has lost the target between the prior invocation and this invocation, or the target was not in range in the previous invocation also. The first case represents a transition between the "acquired" state and the "lost" state. A target alert is generated with the acquired flag set to false to indicate this transition. As will be discussed in the next section, this notification causes the neighboring nodes to update their local state and clear any nonzero reading that may have been associated with this node. Finally, the current reading is saved as oldReading in readiness for the next invocation of this task.

5.5.3   Abstract Task: Leader

The Leader task is the most complex of all three abstract tasks in the ATaG program for object tracking. Indeed, it is the most important task of this ATaG

```
1    package atag.application;
2
3    import atag.runtime.*;
4    import atag.sensor.*;
5    import atag.runtime.config.*;
6    import visualizer.*;
7
8    public class SampleAndThreshold implements Runnable {
9      private TargetAlert m_targetAlert = new TargetAlert();
10     private DataPool m_dataPool;
11     private DataItem m_dataitem;
12     private Config m_myState;
13     private Sensor m_aSensor;
14     private NetworkArchitecture m_networkArchitecture;
15
16     private mGUI m_GUI;
17     private GUIMessage m_guiMessage;
18     private int latestReading;
19     private static int oldReading;
20     private static boolean acquired=false;
21
22     public SampleAndThreshold(DataPool dp, Config myconfig,
23                               NetworkArchitecture t_networkArchitecture,
24                               mGUI t_GUI) {
25       m_aSensor = new Sensor(myconfig.myID(), Constants.ACOUSTIC_SENSOR);
26       m_dataPool = dp;
27       m_myState = myconfig;
28       m_networkArchitecture = t_networkArchitecture;
29       m_GUI = t_GUI;
30     }
31
32     public void run() {
33       try {
34         for (; ; ) {
35           latestReading = m_aSensor.reading();
36           m_dataitem = new DataItem(IDConstants.D_TARGETALERT,
37                                     IDConstants.T_SAMPLEANDTHRESHOLD,
38                                     m_targetAlert);
39           if (latestReading > 0) {
40             m_targetAlert.setDistance(latestReading);
41             m_targetAlert.setAcquired(true);
42             if (!acquired) {
43               acquired = true;
44             }
45             m_dataPool.putData(m_dataitem);
46           } else if (latestReading == 0 && oldReading != 0) {
47             acquired = false;
48             m_targetAlert.setAcquired(false);
49             m_guiMessage.setNodeOutput("Target lost");
50             m_GUI.send(m_guiMessage);
51             m_dataPool.putData(m_dataitem);
52           }
53           oldReading = latestReading;
54
55           Thread.sleep(2000);
56         }
57       }
58       catch (InterruptedException e) {
59         return;
60       }
61     }
```

Figure 5.18   Complete code listing for the SampleAndThreshold task.

program. The SampleAndThreshold task has a relatively simple logic: Periodically sample the acoustic sensor, and if a nonzero (zero) reading is detected, compare it with the earlier reading, but if the reading in the previous invocation was zero (nonzero) produce a TargetAlert data item corresponding to target acquisition (loss). All activity—sampling of the sensor, comparison with previous state, and production of output data item—occurs on the same node. and state maintenance within the task is limited to storing the last read value from the acoustic sensor. The Supervisor task (to be discussed in the next section) is also quite simple and has the same role as the AlarmActuator task in the temperature gradient monitoring application. The role of the Supervisor task is to produce some alarm notification (or perform some other computation) whenever a report of a target location is received from the field in the form of a TargetInfo packet.

The Leader task has a more involved logic than the two other abstract tasks. Input data for this task (TargetAlert) can arrive from any node within a 10-meter radius of the host node that detects the target. As the target moves, the subset of nodes broadcasting the target alerts keeps changing. Also, depending on the speed of movement of the target, its path, and the sampling frequency of the sampling and thresholding task, multiple target alerts can be received from the same nodes while other nodes within a 10-meter radius may be sending no alerts because they are out of range of the object. This complicates state maintenance because readings received from all nodes have to be maintained, including readings from sampling tasks on the same node as the leader. The leader task is responsible for determining if it should generate and transmit the object information to the root node, or if it should depend on leader tasks executing on other nodes that have detected the object to do the same. Ideally, only one of the nodes that have detected the object will elect itself as leader, and the leader task will generate the object information based on readings received from other nodes and send it to the supervisor task on the rot node.

There are some assumptions implicit in the formulation of this ATaG program and specifically in encoding the imperative portion of the Leader task. For instance, if two nodes that have detected the object at the same time have equal sensor readings that are also the maximum of all sensor readings on nodes that have detected the object, the program can lead to duplicate TargetInfo notifications being generated. There is no mechanism in the program for the Leader task to autonomously resolve situations where its own reading and the reading of one or more of its neighboring nodes is the same and is also the maximum of all readings it has received until that instant.

For applications that do not perform any critical in-network actuation or other computation, this duplication could be acceptable. At the supervisor node, all received TargetInfo notifications can be examined for their spatio-temporal origin, and a simple filtering mechanism can be implemented to detect scenarios where two nodes claim "ownership" of the object at the same (or "sufficiently close") timestamp. These issues are not addressed in this simple ATaG program.

Figure 5.19 shows the code for the constructor, member variables, and helper functions for the Leader class. Lines 1–11 should be obvious and have also been discussed in previous sections. The variables in lines 11–19 constitute the state of the Leader task. At initialization, the node's own reading, as stored in the Leader task is set to zero, and the node is also marked as not being the current leader. The myReading variable is used to record the last received reading from the SampleAndThreshold task on the local node (i.e., the same node that is hosting the Leader). The currentLeader is used to record the latest state of this node; a true value indicates that this instance of the Leader is reporting the object information to the root node by electing itself as the node that is closest to the object, based on readings received from all nodes within range of the object.

In lines 27–31, the task gathers the node IDs and coordinates of all neighboring nodes within a distance 210 units from itself. The number 210 is selected arbitrarily in this example. Let d be the sensing range of the acoustic sensor; that is, the object of interest registers on all acoustic sensors in a d unit radius from its current position. Then, the number to be set in lines 29 and 31 is $2d$. The intent is to ensure that the Leader task on a node that is within distance d of the object receives readings from all other nodes that have detected the same target. Since the maximum distance between two nodes that have detected the target is two times the sensing radius, the node can expect to receive TargetAlert notifications from other nodes in a $2d$ radius of that node. In this prototype program, the number is hard-coded into the imperative portion of the task, but this practice is not recommended. The sensing radius should be defined in a Constants class and referred to where required.

Helper functions are defined in lines 35–55. The getReadingCount method returns the number of readings corresponding to distinct neighboring nodes that have been stored by the Leader task at that instant. The maxNeighbor-Reading method returns the maximum reading from among all readings stored by the Leader task at the time the method is invoked. The setNeighbor-Reading accepts an integer reading and node ID, and it sets the reading corresponding to that node ID to the integer value passed to the method.

```
1    package atag.application;
2    import atag.runtime.*;
3    import atag.runtime.config.*;
4    import visualizer.*;
5
6    public class Leader implements Runnable {
7        DataPool m_dataPool;
8        private Config m_myState;
9        private mGUI m_GUI;
10       private GUIMessage m_guiMessage;
11       private NetworkArchitecture m_networkArchitecture;
12
13       private static int[] targetReadings;
14       private static int[] neighborIDs;
15       private static int[][] neighborCoords;
16
17       private static int myReading = 0;
18       private static int acquiredEpoch = 0;    // not used
19       private static boolean currentLeader = false;
20
21       public Leader(DataPool dp, Config myconfig,
22                       NetworkArchitecture t_networkArchitecture,
23                       mGUI t_GUI) {
24           m_dataPool = dp;
25           m_myState = myconfig;
26           m_GUI = t_GUI;
27           m_networkArchitecture = t_networkArchitecture;
28           neighborIDs =
29               m_networkArchitecture.dDistanceNeighborIDs(210);
30           neighborCoords =
31               m_networkArchitecture.dDistanceNeighborCoords(210);
32           targetReadings = new int[neighborIDs.length];
33       }
34
35       private double getReadingCount() {
36           double count = 0;
37           for (int i = 0; i < targetReadings.length; i++)
38               if (targetReadings[i] != 0)
39                   count++;
40           return count;
41       }
42
43       private int maxNeighborReading() {
44           int max = 0;
45           for (int i = 0; i < targetReadings.length; i++)
46               if (targetReadings[i] > max)
47                   max = targetReadings[i];
48           return max;
49       }
50
51       private void setNeighborReading(int nid, int d) {
52           for (int i = 0; i < neighborIDs.length; i++)
53               if (neighborIDs[i] == nid)
54                   targetReadings[i] = d;
55       }
56       ...
57   }
```

Figure 5.19   Constructor, member variables, and helper functions for the Leader task.

The main computation is performed in the `run()` method shown in Figure 5.20. Now, this method is invoked whenever a `TargetAlert` is received at the local data pool. This alert can be generated on the local node, or received from any of the neighboring nodes within the specified radius of that node. The information that can be derived from the `TargetAlert` data item includes (a) the ID and location of the node where the data item originated and (b) the reading of the acoustic sensor at the node. Remember that the `SampleAndThreshold` task creates the alert only when the object has been detected. Hence, whenever the `Leader` receives a target alert, it is assumed that it has been sent by a node that is within range of the object. Whenever the `TargetAlert` is received, the `Leader` task has to determine if sufficient information exists to make a decision on electing itself the leader node (i.e., the node closest to the target at that moment) and transmitting the information to the supervisor node.

Several factors are to be considered while making this decision. The first, and the most obvious factor is whether the reading at the local node is greater than the readings received from neighboring nodes. Note that we do not handle scenarios where two nodes have the same (and maximum) readings. The second factor is what fraction of the neighboring nodes have actually sent the readings. Consider the scenario in Figure 5.21. When the object is at position **O**, it is within the sensing radius of nodes 1, 3, and 4 and is detected by the sampling tasks at those three nodes. Now, each node sends a `TargetAlert` to all nodes in its neighborhood. Hence, node 1 will receive alerts from nodes 3 and 4. Depending on the precise moment when the alerts are generated and the delays in transmitting the alerts over the network, node 1 could receive the reading from node 3 before it receives the reading from node 4. The `Leader` task on node 1 will be invoked when its own sampling task detects the object, and when the alerts are received from nodes 3 and 4. Hence, in its first invocation, the node's own reading is nonzero but it hasn't received any readings from neighbors. Next, when the alert from node 3 is received, it could be less than the node's own reading. At this point, the `Leader` task could potentially compare its reading with that of node 3 and elect itself the leader. Based on the global information as depicted in Figure 5.21, this will be a wrong decision because node 4 is closer to the position **O** and is the rightful leader. Ideally, node 1 will wait for the reading from node 4 to be received and determine that it's own reading is not the maximum. In the actual network, node 1 will have to make this decision based on purely local information.

```
1    public void run () {
2        DataItem t_dataItem = m_dataPool.getData (
3                                 IDConstants.T_LEADER,
4                                 IDConstants.D_TARGETALERT);
5        TargetAlert t_tAlert = null;
6        if (t_dataItem != null) {
7            t_tAlert = (TargetAlert) t_dataItem.core ();
8        }
9
10       if (t_tAlert == null)
11           return;
12
13       int originID = t_dataItem.originID ();
14       if (originID == m_myState.myID ()) {
15           if (t_tAlert.acquired ())
16               myReading = t_tAlert.distance ();
17           else {
18               myReading = 0;
19               return;
20           }
21       } else {
22           if (t_tAlert.acquired ())
23               setNeighborReading(originID, t_tAlert.distance ());
24           else
25               setNeighborReading(originID, 0);
26       }
27
28       if (myReading > maxNeighborReading ()) {
29           if (!currentLeader) {
30               currentLeader = true;
31               System.out.println(m_myState.myID () +":␣REPORTING␣TARGET");
32               TargetInfo m_targetInfo = new TargetInfo (
33                       m_networkArchitecture.myCoords (),
34                       m_myState.myID ());
35               DataItem m_dataitem = new DataItem (IDConstants.
36                       D_TARGETINFO,
37                       IDConstants.T_LEADER, m_targetInfo);
38               m_dataPool.putData(m_dataitem);
39               m_guiMessage = new GUIMessage(m_myState.myID (),
40                                 GUIMessage.GUIM_NODEOUTPUT,
41                                 "");
42               m_guiMessage.setNodeOutput("LEADER");
43               m_GUI.send(m_guiMessage);
44           } else {
45               // do nothing if I am not already the leader
46           }
47       } else {
48           if (currentLeader) {
49               m_guiMessage = new GUIMessage(m_myState.myID (),
50                                 GUIMessage.GUIM_NODEOUTPUT,
51                                 "");
52               m_guiMessage.setNodeOutput("EXLEADER");
53               m_GUI.send(m_guiMessage);
54               currentLeader = false;
55           }
56       }
57       return;
58   }
```

Figure 5.20 The run() routine of the Leader task.

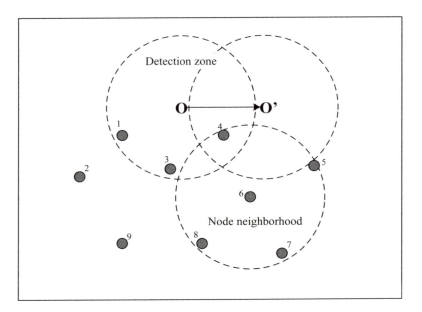

Figure 5.21 `TargetAlert` received from only one neighbor.

We do not propose the "right" solution to this problem and merely explain the logic of our particular implementation of the `Leader` task as shown by the listing in Figure 5.20.

When the `TargetAlert` is consumed by the node, the following processing occurs:

1. Lines 13–26: The origin of the data item is checked to determine if it is produced by the local sampler task or has arrived from one of the neighboring nodes. If the data item is local and the `acquired` flag is set, the `Leader` task records the local reading in the `myReading` variable. If the `acquired` flag is set to false, it means that the local node has lost the object; that is, the object is out of sensing range of the node. In that case, the `myReading` variable is set to zero. If the data item is not local, a similar process is carried out and the neighbor's reading is recorded in the suitable array entry or set to zero if the alert indicates that the target was lost.

2. Lines 28–46: At this stage, the received reading has been stored in the suitable variable. Now, the node's local reading is compared with the maximum among all readings from neighboring nodes. If the local

reading is greater than that received from the neighbors, the node first determines if it has already elected itself the leader in a previous invocation of this task. If the node is the current leader, no action is taken. If the node is not the current leader, it first declares itself the leader by setting the appropriate state variable. This state is maintained to avoid sending repeated, duplicate messages to the supervisor node (and to the visualization front end). Next, the TargetInfo data item is created. In this implementation, this data item merely records the ID of the node that has elected itself the leader by virtue of being closest to the object based on information received till that time. This data item is added to the data pool and a message is sent to the visualization interface.

3. Lines 47–56: If the local reading is not greater than the maximum of all readings received from neighboring nodes, it means that the node is clearly not the leader. If the node was the leader in the previous invocation, the state is changed to false and the corresponding message is sent to the visualization interface.

Note that this implementation does not have to worry about old readings from neighboring nodes being preserved as part of the state maintained by the Leader and possibly affecting its logic adversely. This is because the ATaG program ensures that when the node loses a target (i.e., the acoustic sensor reading becomes zero), it sends out the corresponding message to all nodes in its neighborhood. This effectively sets to zero the reading associated with that node in all the Leader tasks hosted in its neighborhood.

5.5.4   Abstract Task: Supervisor

The code listing for the Supervisor task is shown in Figure 5.22. The purpose of this task is the same as that of the AlarmActuator task in the temperature gradient monitoring application. Briefly, it receives all data items of type TargetInfo created anywhere in the network. When an instance of such a data item is received, it determines its origin and determines the location of the object of interest in the sensor network. In this implementation, this task sends a message to the visualization interface and logs the receipt of this message.

5.6   APPLICATION COMPOSITION

Each ATaG program thus defined forms part of a library of behaviors that can be reused in other applications. Figure 5.25 shows a library of ATaG

```
package atag.application;

import atag.runtime.*;
import atag.runtime.config.*;
import visualizer.*;

public class Supervisor implements Runnable {
  DataPool m_dataPool;
  private Config m_myState;
  private mGUI m_GUI;
  private GUIMessage m_guiMessage;
  private NetworkArchitecture m_networkArchitecture;
  private static int lastX = -1;
  private static int lastY = -1;

  public Supervisor(DataPool dp, Config myconfig,
                    NetworkArchitecture t_networkArchitecture,
                    mGUI t_GUI) {
    m_dataPool = dp;
    m_myState = myconfig;
    m_networkArchitecture = t_networkArchitecture;
    m_GUI = t_GUI;
  }

  public void run() {
    DataItem t_dataItem = m_dataPool.getData(
                              IDConstants.T_SUPERVISOR,
                              IDConstants.D_TARGETINFO);
    TargetInfo t_targetInfo = null;
    if (t_dataItem != null) {
      t_targetInfo = (TargetInfo) t_dataItem.core();
    }

    // START OF USER CODE
    int[] tLoc = t_targetInfo.coords();
    int currX = tLoc[0];
    int currY = tLoc[1];
    int nodeid = t_targetInfo.reportingNode();
    if (currX != lastX || currY != lastY) {
      lastX = currX;
      lastY = currY;
      m_guiMessage = new GUIMessage(m_myState.myID(),
                              GUIMessage.GUIM_NODEOUTPUT, "");
      m_guiMessage.setNodeOutput("Node " + nodeid + " @ " +
                              currX+","+currY+" reports object");
      m_GUI.send(m_guiMessage);
    }
  }
  // END OF USER CODE
}
```

Figure 5.22   Complete code listing for the Supervisor task.

programs consisting of three behaviors: object tracking, gradient monitoring, and centralized data collection. Currently, the building blocks for each behavior are abstract tasks, data, and channels that are indicated by directed arrows between tasks and data items. This modeling paradigm developed for prototyping purposes is not ideal because some behaviors might include other behaviors too; in other words, the building blocks provided to the programmer should include abstract tasks, abstract data, and pointers (references) to other behaviors in the library. In the gradient monitoring program of Figure 5.6, notice that the pattern of communication implied by the Monitor, Fire, and AlarmActuator subgraph is centralized data collection. Similarly, the pattern of communication implied by LeaderElect, TargetInfo, and Supervisor in the object tracking program of Figure 5.7 is also centralized data collection. The next version of the application modeling paradigm for ATaG will allow the programmer to integrate existing behaviors (such as the centralized data collection behavior shown as CentralizedDC in Figure 5.25) into other behaviors to maximize reuse. This composition is illustrated in Figure 5.26.

The next version of the modeling paradigm will allow the programmer to perform such composition through appropriate building blocks in the GME interface.

Next, the target network is described by instantiating a *Deployment* model and setting the parameter values to match the target deployment. As shown in the metamodel of Figure 4.4 a *Deployment* consists of one or more atoms of type *SensorNode*. Node-level parameters are specified as attributes of *SensorNode*, while network-level parameters are specified for the model *Deployment*. The set of attributes can be easily increased or otherwise modified, depending on the information required by the particular tools to be driven through the GME framework. Figures 5.23 and 5.24 show the library of deployment descriptions and the details of one particular 9-node deployment respectively. Network-level and node-level parameters for this example are shown in the lower right sections of the GME windows.

The library of ATaG programs in GME consists only of the declarative portions—that is, the number of abstract tasks, data, and channels, and their annotations. The code associated with each abstract task is to be provided separately as a Java class that extends the UserTask class of DART (see Section 3.3.2). The developer of an ATaG behavior that is contributed to the library is also expected to provide the Java classes associated with the abstract tasks.

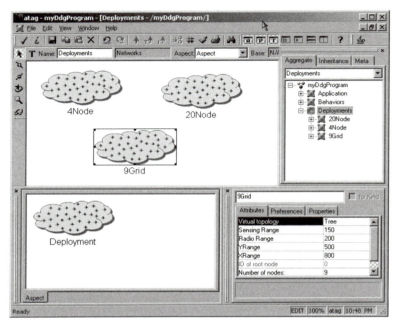

Figure 5.23 GME model: A library of deployments.

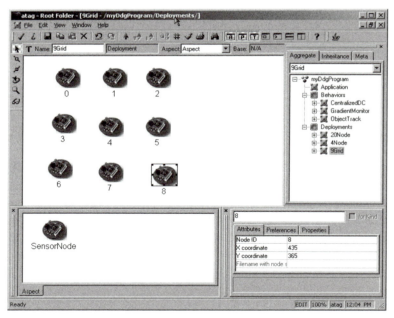

Figure 5.24 GME model: A network of 9 nodes.

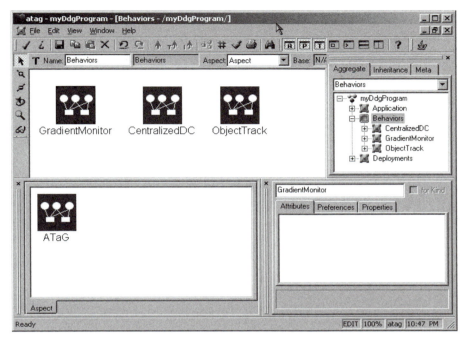

Figure 5.25   GME model: Library of ATaG programs (behaviors).

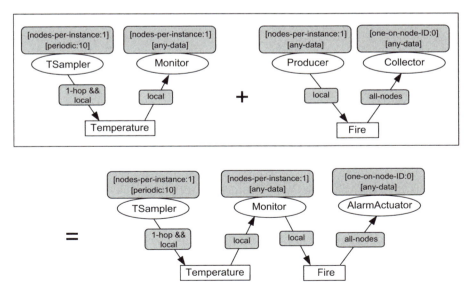

Figure 5.26   Composing ATaG programs from existing libraries.

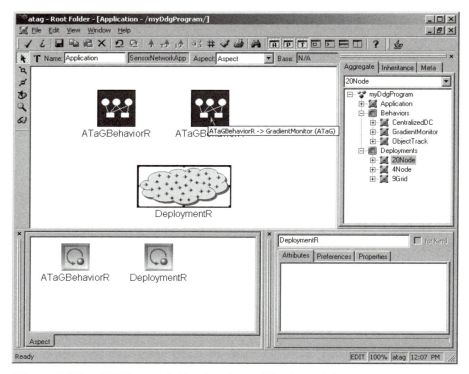

Figure 5.27   GME model: Top level specification of the application as a set of behaviors mapped onto one target deployment.

Given the library of ATaG programs and the library of deployment descriptions, defining and synthesizing a networked sensing application is straightforward. The application is defined as an instance of the *SensorNetworkApp* model (Figure 4.1) that consists of one or more references (pointers) to ATaG programs and one reference to a deployment description.

Figure 5.27 is an ATaG program that contains two behaviors from the library: object tracking and gradient monitoring. This program is specified by instantiating one `ATaGBehaviorR` reference for each behavior, linking each reference to its target behavior, instantiating one `DeploymentR` reference to the target deployment description, and linking it to the desired 20-node deployment. Since the two component behaviors of the program are part of the library, the application code will also be available. Hence, the application developer is not required to write any new code or draw any new ATaG diagrams. Such an interface can be used by end users who have no expertise or knowledge of ATaG, Java, or the lower-level aspects of sensor networking.

```
 1   package atag.application;
 2
 3   /* Auto-generated */
 4
 5   public class IDConstants {
 6           public static final int T_TSAMPLER = 0;
 7           public static final int T_ALARMACTUATOR = 1;
 8           public static final int T_MONITOR = 2;
 9           public static final int T_SUPERVISOR = 3;
10           public static final int T_LEADER = 4;
11           public static final int T_SAMPLEANDTHRESHOLD = 5;
12           public static final int D_FIRE = 0;
13           public static final int D_TEMPERATURE = 1;
14           public static final int D_TARGETINFO = 2;
15           public static final int D_TARGETALERT = 3;
16   }
```

Figure 5.28   The automatically generated IDConstants class.

5.7   SOFTWARE SYNTHESIS

Translation of placement annotations and channel annotations, and the general of skeleton code for abstract tasks and data items was discussed in Section 4.4. In this section, we show the specific artifacts created by the ATaG programming system for the two ATaG programs discussed in earlier sections.

Figure 5.28 shows the IDConstants class that is generated automatically. In the current implementation, each abstract task is required to have a unique integer identifier and so is every abstract data item. The identifiers are used by the runtime system to refer to (index) the tasks and data items. The assignment of identifiers to tasks and data items is done for the entire application, which itself might consist of independently written ATaG programs. Hence, it is impossible to hard-code these identifiers as task and data IDs while writing the individual programs. On the other hand, these identifiers are required as arguments to the get() and put() functions of the data pool and some other methods that are used by the application-level code. To allow ATaG programmers to write programs without worrying about the identifier assignment, we permit the use of constants—prefixed by a T_ for abstract tasks and a D_ for abstract data items—in the code, instead of the actual integers. When the overall application is composed, the IDConstants class is generated that associates the constants with integers.

The only code in the runtime system that is generated automatically is a portion of the constructor of the AtagManager class that instantiates the abstract task and channel declarations. This automatically generated code fragment for our application is shown in Figure 5.29.

```
1   // ************ START OF AUTO-GENERATED CODE
2   numTaskDecls = 6;
3   taskDecls.add(IDConstants.T_TSAMPLER,
4           new TaskDeclaration(IDConstants.T_TSAMPLER,
5               new TSampler(m_dataPool, m_config,
6                   m_networkArchitecture, m_GUI),
7           Thread.MAX_PRIORITY-0, "NODES PER INSTANCE",
8           false, 1, "PERIODIC", 1, true));
9   taskDecls.add(IDConstants.T_ALARMACTUATOR,
10          new TaskDeclaration(IDConstants.T_ALARMACTUATOR,
11              new AlarmActuator(m_dataPool, m_config,
12                  m_networkArchitecture, m_GUI),
13          Thread.MAX_PRIORITY-5, "ONE INSTANCE ON NODE ID",
14          false, 0, "ANYDATA", 3600, false));
15  taskDecls.add(IDConstants.T_MONITOR,
16          new TaskDeclaration(IDConstants.T_MONITOR,
17              new Monitor(m_dataPool, m_config,
18                  m_networkArchitecture, m_GUI),
19          Thread.MAX_PRIORITY-4, "NODES PER INSTANCE",
20          false, 1, "ANYDATA", 2, true));
21  taskDecls.add(IDConstants.T_SUPERVISOR,
22          new TaskDeclaration(IDConstants.T_SUPERVISOR,
23              new Supervisor(m_dataPool, m_config,
24                  m_networkArchitecture, m_GUI),
25          Thread.MAX_PRIORITY-2, "ONE INSTANCE ON NODE ID",
26          false, 0, "ANYDATA", 3600, false));
27  taskDecls.add(IDConstants.T_LEADER,
28          new TaskDeclaration(IDConstants.T_LEADER,
29              new Leader(m_dataPool, m_config,
30                  m_networkArchitecture, m_GUI),
31          Thread.MAX_PRIORITY-1, "NODES PER INSTANCE",
32          false, 1, "ANYDATA", 3600, false));
33  taskDecls.add(IDConstants.T_SAMPLEANDTHRESHOLD,
34          new TaskDeclaration(IDConstants.T_SAMPLEANDTHRESHOLD,
35              new SampleAndThreshold(m_dataPool, m_config,
36                  m_networkArchitecture, m_GUI),
37          Thread.MAX_PRIORITY-0, "NODES PER INSTANCE",
38          false, 1, "PERIODIC", 1, true));
39
40  numChannelDecls = 8;
41  channelDecls.add(0, new ChannelDeclaration(IDConstants.T_MONITOR,
42          IDConstants.D_TEMPERATURE, "INPUT", false, "push", "", 0));
43  channelDecls.add(1, new ChannelDeclaration(IDConstants.T_ALARMACTUATOR,
44          IDConstants.D_FIRE, "INPUT", false, "push", "ALLNODES", 0));
45  channelDecls.add(2, new ChannelDeclaration(IDConstants.T_TSAMPLER,
46          IDConstants.D_TEMPERATURE, "OUTPUT", true, "push",
47          "NEIGHBORHOP", 1));
48  channelDecls.add(3, new ChannelDeclaration(IDConstants.T_MONITOR,
49          IDConstants.D_FIRE, "OUTPUT", true, "push", "", 0));
50  channelDecls.add(4, new ChannelDeclaration(IDConstants.T_LEADER,
51          IDConstants.D_TARGETALERT, "INPUT", false, "push", "", 0));
52  channelDecls.add(5, new ChannelDeclaration(IDConstants.T_SUPERVISOR,
53          IDConstants.D_TARGETINFO, "INPUT", false, "push",
54          "ALLNODES", 0));
55  channelDecls.add(6, new ChannelDeclaration(IDConstants.T_LEADER,
56          IDConstants.D_TARGETINFO, "OUTPUT", true, "push", "", 0));
57  channelDecls.add(7, new ChannelDeclaration(
58          IDConstants.T_SAMPLEANDTHRESHOLD, IDConstants.D_TARGETALERT,
59          "OUTPUT", true, "push",
60          "NEIGHBORDISTANCE", 300));
61  }
62  // ************ END OF AUTO-GENERATED CODE
```

Figure 5.29   The automatically generated portion of the `AtaGManager` constructor class.

```
-myID 0 -ndata 4 -ntasks 6 -hopscope 0 -distancescope 0
-assignedtasks 0 1 2 3 4 5 -senddata 0 0 -senddata 2 0 -end

-myID 1 -ndata 4 -ntasks 6 -hopscope 0 -distancescope 0
-assignedtasks 0 2 4 5 -senddata 0 0 -senddata 2 0 -end
```

Figure 5.30   Sample configuration files for nodes 0 and 1 respectively.

Finally, each node is provided with a configuration file that is read by the runtime system at initialization. The configuration file includes the node ID, the total number of abstract tasks and abstract data items, the hop scope and distance scope parameters, the tasks assigned to that node, and any directives related to data transmission to a hard-coded location.

In our example applications, the TSampler, SampleAndThreshold, Monitor, and Leader tasks are to be mapped onto every node in the system. The IDs of these tasks as shown in the IDConstants class are 0, 5, 2, and 4, respectively. Hence, the configuration file for each node will contain these numbers in the assigned tasks section. Configuration files for the root node (node with ID 0) and for a non-root node are shown in Figure 5.30.

As shown in the figure, the configuration file for node 0 contains all tasks (including the AlarmActuator and Supervisor tasks with IDs 1 and 3 respectively, as well as the other four tasks). The non-root node does not host tasks 1 and 3. The hopscope and distancescope parameters are not supported in the current version of DART, hence the corresponding entries are zero. If support for this feature had existed, the hopscope parameter would be 1 in light of the output channel annotation for the TSampler task, and the distancescope parameter would be the distance specified on the output channel of the SampleAndThreshold task.

As the last step in the application development process, the entire software system—including the runtime system modules and application-level tasks—has to be compiled. For simulation and visualization, independent processes have to be launched for each simulated node and the configuration file is provided as a parameter to customize the behavior of the individual processes.

CHAPTER 6

CONCLUDING REMARKS

The Abstract Task Graph is an attempt at defining a programming model and methodology that enables application developers to focus on the high level structure of collaborative computation without worrying about the details of the target sensor network deployment. It is based on the belief that ease of application development will ultimately determine the penetration of networked sensor systems into everyday life, and it can be achieved not just by defining more and more protocols for different aspects of networked sensing but by also providing frameworks where a selection of existing protocols can be packaged and provided as services through an integrated application development environment.

In the following two sections, we comment on the role of ATaG as (a) a framework for defining architecture-independent programming languages for specific application domains and (b) an extensible framework for integrating a variety of compilation and software synthesis tools for multiple platforms and driving their execution from a single application development environment.

Architecture-Independent Programming for Wireless Sensor Networks
By Amol B. Bakshi, Viktor K. Prasanna **175**

6.1 A FRAMEWORK FOR DOMAIN-SPECIFIC APPLICATION DEVELOPMENT

ATaG is based on two concepts. The first is data-driven computing, which provides a natural mental model for specifying reactive behaviors and has other significant benefits from a software development perspective such as composability and reusability. The second concept, which is the key to architecture independence at the network level, is the use of declarative task and channel annotations to specify the placement of functionalities and the patterns of interaction between functionalities.

The task and channel annotations currently defined for ATaG and summarized in Tables 2.1 and 2.2 are merely meant to illustrate the power of declarative programming with ATaG. The choice of annotations was influenced by our desire to express patterns of interaction that form the building blocks of in-network computation in oft-cited behaviors such as object tracking and environment monitoring. The annotations are not intended to be an exhaustive list, and we expect that they will be modified to suit the particular application domain and the services available in the target deployment. For instance, the current set of task annotations allows placement based on node IDs or locations. This can be generalized to placement based on *context labels*. The idea of context labels is employed in EnviroTrack [1] as a mechanism to address sensor nodes and also to host context-specific computation. The idea behind context labels is to allow the user to specify dynamic behaviors based on the current state of a node. The fraction of total energy reserves currently remaining in the node can be considered as a context. This context can be used as a task annotation to specify alternate implementations of the same task and tag each implementation with the context of its invocation. This can be used to adapt the computation to the amount of available energy and provide graceful degradation of functionality where possible. Other interpretations of the context of a node can be used to trigger specific behaviors only if other behaviors are activated on neighboring nodes. For instance, the programmer could want task A to start executing on a node only when at least 50% of its 1-hop neighborhood are executing task B. This will require a context label for each node that indicates whether task B is executing on that node, and a context label that indicates whether 50% of the node's 1-hop neighborhood has the context label indicating task B.

The point of these examples is to show that ATaG can be customized to a particular domain by defining task and channel annotations relevant to that domain. The requirement for defining a new domain-specific annotation is the existence of a mechanism to translate the annotation into a set of parameters used to customize DART, along with the availability of all the relevant information in the network model provided to the compiler.

6.2 A FRAMEWORK FOR COMPILATION AND SOFTWARE SYNTHESIS

Just as the extensible set of ATaG annotations form a framework for domain-specific customization of the declarative part of ATaG, the component-based design of DART can be considered to be a framework for integrating a variety of protocols proposed for sensor network applications. The purpose of this integration is to ultimately provide an end-to-end application development methodology that allows an application developer to use these protocols (explicitly or implicitly) for a real-world application without necessarily knowing the details of their implementation, or even of their existence.

A critical part of this end-to-end methodology that is only superficially addressed in this work is the ATaG compiler. The high-level concept of compilation of a networked sensing application can be defined as the translation of a service-oriented specification or a macroprogramming language into an 'equivalent' distributed software system to be deployed on a target network. The exact algorithms used for compilation, the structure of the compilation process, and the scope for compile-time and runtime optimization, however, depends entirely on the particular programming model and runtime system.

The contribution of ATaG and DART and, to some extent, of the GME-based visual programming and software synthesis environment is to create a framework for compilation and software synthesis in the following sense. Each annotation (or a group of annotations) has a well-defined association with a particular module or configuration parameter in the DART design. For instance, the result of compiling the task annotation *nodes-per-instance: k* for some abstract task T is that approximately $\frac{1}{k}$ of the `AtagManager` modules in the system will have the assignment flag for task T set to `true`. Channel annotations are also suitably encoded into each node as DART configuration parameters. Every such translation of a task and channel annotation into configuration parameters for DART on some or all nodes in the network can be considered as an independent compilation problem. For instance, the issue of optimal sensing coverage has been the focus of much research in distributed sensing. A version of the coverage problem of special interest in the context of ATaG is the static or dynamic selection of a set of sensors of a particular type, from among all sensors of that type in the network, such that the degree of coverage desired by the application developer is guaranteed with high probability. In the ATaG model, the selection of sensors could effectively translate into the selection of a set of nodes on which the sensing tasks (which are abstract tasks in the graphs) will be instantiated. The job of the compiler in this case is to interpret the high-level intent of the programmer as specified through suitably defined task annotations and assign the sensing tasks to a particular set of nodes. The algorithm used to select this set of nodes will reflect the quality of the compilation by affecting the communication and computation cost that is engendered in the deployment.

The choice of the Generic Modeling Enviornment (GME) for providing the visual programming interface as well as integrating the different tools for software synthesis, simulation, etc., is particularly felicitous from the perspective of the compilation problem. GME allows plug-and-play integration of software components called model interpreters. Each model interpreter, when invoked, can access all information about the current model which, in our domain, includes the library of behaviors, deployments, and the application to be synthesized. A model interpreter for synthesizing the code skeletons for abstract tasks and data items inspects the I/O relationships between tasks and data to generate the suitable get() or put() calls, the names of the tasks and data items to generate the names of the java classes, and the firing rules for the abstract tasks to generate a suitably timed loop for periodic execution if specified by the firing rule. Other model interpreters will read the model information relevant to their own specific function. The compiler is just another (set of) model interpreter that reads the relevant annotations from the model database and performs the appropriate transformations either on the model itself or on external objects such as the DART code for a particular node. This flexibility also makes it possible for the same programming environment to seamlessly support a set of compilers and software synthesizers, each for a different target platform.

In summary, the contribution of ATaG is the definition of an extensible language, runtime system, and compilation framework that can be tailored to different application domains, network architectures, performance metrics, and sensor node platforms, depending on the requirements of the end user. The work described in this document is a specific instance of this general framework.

REFERENCES

1. T. Abdelzaher, B. Blum, Q. Cao, D. Evans, J. George, S. George, T. He, L. Luo, S. Son, R. Stoleru, J. Stankovic, and A. Wood. EnviroTrack: An environmental programming model for tracking applications in distributed sensor networks. In *Proceedings of International Conference on Distributed Computing Systems (ICDCS)*, 2004.

2. T. F. Abdelzaher and K. G. Shin. Optimal combined task and message scheduling in distributed real-time systems. In *16th IEEE Real-Time Systems Symposium*, pages 162–171, December 1995.

3. I. F. Akyildiz, W. Su, Y. Sankarasubramaniam, and E. Cayirci. Wireless sensor networks: A survey. *Computer Networks*, 38:393–422, 2002.

4. S. Ali, A. A. Maciejewski, H. J. Siegel, and J.-K. Kim. Robust resource allocation for sensor–actuator distributed computing systems. In *International Conference on Parallel Processing (ICPP)*, 2004.

5. Arvind and R. A. Iannucci. Two fundamental issues in multiprocessing: The data flow solution. Computation Structures Group Memo 226-2, Laboratory for Computer Science, Massachusetts Institute of Technology, July 1983.

Architecture-Independent Programming for Wireless Sensor Networks   **179**
By Amol B. Bakshi, Viktor K. Prasanna
Copyright © 2008 John Wiley & Sons, Inc.

6. A. Bakshi, V. K. Prasanna, J. Reich, and D. Larner. The abstract task graph: A methodology for architecture-independent programming of networked sensor systems. In *Workshop on End-to-End Sense-and-Respond Systems (EESR)*, June 2005.

7. A. Bakshi, M. Singh, and V. K. Prasanna. Constructing topographic maps in networked sensor systems. In *Algorithm for Wireless And mobile Networks (A-SWAN)*, August 2004.

8. H. E. Bal, J. G. Steiner, and A. S. Tanenbaum. Programming languages for distributed computing systems. *ACM Computing Surveys*, 21(3):261–322, September 1989.

9. G. Banavar, J. Beck, E. Gluzberg, J. Munson, J. Sussman, and D. Zukowski. Challenges: An Application Model for Pervasive Computing. In *6th Annual ACM/IEEE International Conference on Mobile Computing and Networking*, 2000.

10. K. Bondalapati and V. K. Prasanna. Dynamic precision management for loop computations on reconfigurable architectures. In *IEEE Symposium on Field-Programmable Custom Computing Machines (FCCM)*.

11. N. Busi, A. Rowstron, and G. Zavattaro. State- and event-based reactive programming in shared dataspaces. In *Proceedings of International Conference on Coordination Models and Languages (COORDINATION'02)*, number 2315 in Lecture Notes in Computer Science, pages 111–124, Springer-Verlag, Berlin, 2002.

12. I. Chatzigiannakis, G. Mylonas, and S. Nikoletseas. jWebDust: A Java-based generic application environment for wireless sensor networks. In *International Conference on Distributed Computing in Sensor Systems (DCOSS)*, June 2005.

13. E. Cheong and J. Liu. galsC: A language for event-driven embedded systems. In *Proceedings of Design, Automation and Test in Europe (DATE)*, 2005.

14. C. Curino, M. Giani, M. Giorgetta, A. Giusti, G. P. Picco, and A. L. Murphy. Tiny Lime: Bridging mobile and sensor networks through middleware. In *3rd IEEE International Conference on Pervasive Computing and Communications*, 2005.

15. J. Elson and D. Estrin. Time synchronization in wireless sensor networks. In *International Parallel and Distributed Processing Symposium (IPDPS), Workshop on Parallel and Distributed Computing Issues in Wireless and Mobile Computing*, April 2001.

16. J. Elson, L. Girod, and D. Estrin. Fine-grained network time synchronization using reference broadcasts. In *Proc. of the Fifth Symposium on Operating Systems Design and Implementation (OSDI)*, December 2002.

17. D. Estrin, D. Culler, K. Pister, and G. Sukhatme. Connecting the physical world with pervasive networks. *IEEE Pervasive Computing*, pages 59–69, 2002.

18. D. Ganesan, A. Cerpa, Y. Yu, W. Ye, J. Zhao, and D. Estrin. Networking issues in wireless sensor networks. *Journal of Parallel and Distributed Computing (JPDC)*, 64(7):799–814, July 2004.

19. D. Gay, P. Levis, R. von Behren, M. Welsh, E. Brewer, and D. Culler. The nesC language: A holistic approach to networked embedded systems. In *Proceedings of Programming Language Design and Implementation (PLDI)*, 2003.

20. D. Gelernter. Generative communication in Linda. *ACM Transactions on Programming Languages and Systems*, 7(1):80–112, 1985.

21. The Generic Modeling Environment, http://www.isis.vanderbilt.edu/projects/gme.

22. R. Govindan. Data-centric routing and storage in sensor networks. In *Wireless Sensor Networks*, T. Znati, K. Sivalingam, and C. S. Raghavendra, editors, Kluwer Academic Publishers, Boston, 2004.

23. R. Gummadi, O. Gnawali, and R. Govindan. Macro-programming wireless sensor networks using kairos. In *International Conference on Distributed Computing in Sensor Systems (DCOSS)*, June 2005.

24. D. Harel and A. Pnueli. On the development of reactive systems. In K. R. Apt (editor), *Logics and Models of Concurrent Systems,* vol. F-13 of NATO ASI Series, pages 477–498, Springer-Verlag, New York, 1985.

25. S. Haridi, P. Van Roy, P. Brand, and C. Schulte. Programming languages for distributed applications. *New Generation Computing*, 16(3):223–261, 1998.

26. W. B. Heinzelman, A. L. Murphy, H. S. Carvalho, and M. A. Perillo. Middleware to support sensor network applications. *IEEE Network*, January 2004.

27. J. Hill, R. Szewczyk, A. Woo, S. Hollar, D. Culler, and K. Pister. System architecture directions for networked sensors. In *9th ACM International Conference on Architectural Support for Programming Languages and Operating Systems*, 2000.

28. O. Holder, I. Ben-Shaul, and H. Gazit. Dynamic layout of distributed applications in FarGo. In *21st International Conference Software Engineering*, 1999.

29. B. Hong and V. K. Prasanna. Constrained flow optimization with applications to data gathering in sensor networks. In *First International Workshop on Algorithmic Aspects of Wireless Sensor Networks (ALGOSENSORS)*, July 2004.

30. B. Hong and V. K. Prasanna. Optimizing system life time for data gathering in networked sensor systems. In *AlgorithmS for Wireless and Ad-hoc Networks (A-SWAN) (Held in conjunction with MobiQuitous 2004)*, August 2004.

31. S. S. Iyengar and R. R. Brooks, editors. *Distributed Sensor Networks*, Chapman & Hall/CRC, Boca Raton, December 2004.

32. S. S. Iyengar and L. Prasad. A general computational framework for distributed sensing and fault-tolerant sensor integration. *IEEE Transactions on Systems, Man and Cybernetics*, 25(4):643–650, April 1995.

33. B. Karp and H. T. Kung. GPSR: Greedy perimeter stateless routing for wireless networks. In *Proceedings of ACM/IEEE MobiCom*, August 2000.

34. D. L. Larner. A distributed, operating system based, blackboard architecture for real-time control. In *International Conference on Industrial and Engineering Applications of Artificial Intelligence and Expert Systems*, 1990.

35. J. Liu, M. Chu, J. Liu, J. Reich, and F. Zhao. State-centric programming for sensor–actuator network systems. In *IEEE Pervasive Computing*, 2003.

36. J. Liu and F. Zhao. Towards service-oriented networked embedded computing. Technical Report MSR-TR-2005-28, Microsoft Research, February 2005.

37. T. Liu and M. Martonosi. Impala: A middleware system for managing autonomic, parallel sensor systems. In *ACM SIGPLAN Symposium on Principles and Practice of Parallel Programming*, 2003.

38. S. Madden, R. Szewczyk, M. Franklin, and D. Culler. Supporting aggregate queries over ad-hoc wireless sensor networks. In *Workshop on Mobile Computing and Systems Applications*, 2002.

39. uC/OS-II RTOS, http://www.ucos-ii.com/.

40. B. Nath and D. Niculescu. Routing on a curve. In *HOTNETS-I*, October 2002.

41. N. Bulusu, J. Heidemann, and D. Estrin. Gps-less low cost outdoor localization for very small devices. *IEEE Personal Communications Magazine*, pages 28–34, March 2000.

42. R. Newton and M. Welsh. Region streams: Functional macroprogramming for sensor networks. In *1st International Workshop on Data Management for Sensor Networks (DMSN)*, 2004.

43. P. Nii. The blackboard model of problem solving. *AI Magazine*, 7(2), 1986.

44. G. J. Pottie and W. J. Kaiser. Wireless integrated network sensors. *Communications of the ACM*, 43(5):51–58, 2000.

45. K. Ramamritham. Allocation and scheduling of complex periodic tasks. In *International Conference on Distributed Computing Systems*, pages 108–115, 1990.

46. R. S. Ramanujan, J. C. Bonney, K. J. Thurber, R. Jha, and H. J. Siegel. A framework for automated software partitioning and mapping for distributed multiprocessors. In *2nd International Symposium on Parallel Architectures, Algorithms, and Networks*, pages 138–145, June 1996.

47. A. Rao, C. Papadimitriou, S. Shenker, and I. Stoica. Geographic routing without location information. In *Proceedings of the 9th Annual International Conference on Mobile Computing and Networking*, pages 96–108, 2003.

48. Real Time Specification for Java, http://www.rtj.org/

49. Real Time Specification for Java, http://www.rtsj.org/

50. Stargate: A PlatformX project, http://platformx.sourceforge.net/.

51. C. Szyperski. *Component-Oriented Software, Beyond Object-Oriented Programming*. Addison-Wesley, Reading, MA, 1997.

52. V. D. Tran, L. Hluchy, and G. T. Nguyen. Data driven graph: A parallel program model for scheduling. In *Proceedings, 12th International Workshop on Languages and Compilers for Parallel Computing*, pages 494–497, 1999.

53. M. Turon and J. Suh. MOTE-VIEW: A sensor network monitoring and management tool. In *2nd IEEE Workshop on Embedded Network Sensors (EmNets)*, May 2005.

54. T. von Eicken, D. E. Culler, S. C. Goldstein, and K. E. Schauser. Active messages: A mechanism for integrated communication and computation. In *19th Annual International Symposium on Computer Architecture*, pages 256–266, 1992.

55. M. Welsh and G. Mainland. Programming sensor networks using abstract regions. In *First USENIX/ACM Symposium on Networked Systems Design and Implementation (NSDI)*, March 2004.

56. K. Whitehouse, C. Sharp, E. Brewer, and D. Culler. Hood: a neighborhood abstraction for sensor networks. In *2nd International Conference on Mobile Systems, Applications, and Services*, 2004.

57. K. Whitehouse, F. Zhao, and J. Liu. Semantic streams: a framework for declarative queries and automatic data interpretation. Technical Report MSR-TR-2005-45, Microsoft Research, April 2005.

58. D. Wu, B. M. Al-Hashimi, and P. Eles. Scheduling and mapping of conditional task graphs for the synthesis of low power embedded systems. In *Proceedings of Design, Automation and Test in Europe (DATE)*, 2003.

59. T. Yang and C. Fu. Heuristic algorithms for scheduling iterative task computations on distributed memory machines. *IEEE Transactions on Parallel and Distributed Systems*, 8(6), June 1997.

60. W. Ye, J. Heidemann, and D. Estrin. An energy-efficient MAC protocol for wireless sensor networks. Technical Report ISI-TR-543, USC/ISI, 2001.

61. Y. Yu, B. Krishnamachari, and V. K. Prasanna. Energy-latency tradeoffs for data gathering in wireless sensor networks. In *Proceedings of INFOCOM*, 2004.

62. Y. Yu, B. Krishnamachari, and V. K. Prasanna. Issues in designing middleware for wireless sensor networks. *IEEE Network*, 18(1), 2004.

63. F. Zambonelli and M. Mamei. Spatial computing: A recipe for self-organization in distributed computing scenarios. In *International Workshop on Self-* Properties in Complex Information Systems*, 2004.

64. J. Zhao, R. Govindan, and D. Estrin. Computing aggregates for monitoring wireless sensor networks. In *International Conference on Communications (ICC), Workshop on Sensor Network Protocols and Applications*, May 2003.

INDEX

μC/OS-II, 99

A

abstract
    channel, 30, 31
    data, 30, 31
    task, 30, 31
abstract channel, 30, 31, 33
abstract data, 30, 31
abstract data items, 143
abstract declarations, 30
abstract task, 32, 75
all-data task, 47
annotations, 30
any-data task, 47
application composition, 165
architecture
    Blackboard, 14
    Harvard, 26
architecture-independent programming, 175
ATaG, 12
    Abstract Task Graph, 16

ATaG behavior, 112, 119
ATaG programs
    libraries, 109
ATaG simulator, 121, 127
AtagManager, 82
attribute-based task placement, 37
automatic software synthesis, 117

B

Blackboard architecture, 14

C

case study, 135
ChannelDeclaration, 72
channels
    input, 112
    output, 112
code placement, 34
code skeletons, 114, 119
communication, 12

Architecture-Independent Programming for Wireless Sensor Networks
By Amol B. Bakshi, Viktor K. Prasanna
Copyright © 2008 John Wiley & Sons, Inc.